IMAGES
of America

COVENTRY

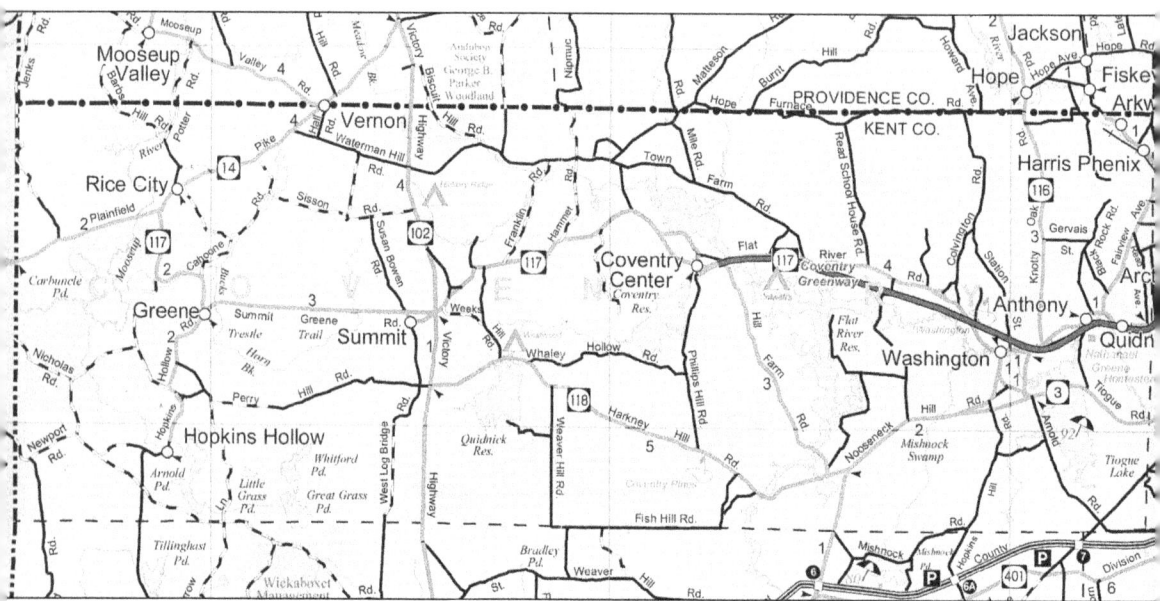

This 2012 Rhode Island state map of Coventry shows the 10 major villages of the town covered in this book. They are, from west to east, Rice City, Greene, Hopkins Hollow, Summit, Coventry Center (originally Coventry Centre), Washington, Anthony, Quidnick, Harris, and Arkwright. (Courtesy of the author's collection.)

ON THE COVER: A small group of bicyclists is out for an afternoon ride in Coventry in the late 1800s. Zilpha W. Foster and her husband, Charles A. Foster, are on the far left and third from the left, respectively. (Courtesy of Coventry Historical Society.)

IMAGES
of America

COVENTRY

Raymond A. Wolf

ARCADIA
PUBLISHING

Published by Arcadia Publishing
Charleston, South Carolina

Library of Congress Control Number: 2013935793

For all general information, please contact Arcadia Publishing:
Telephone 843-853-2070
Fax 843-853-0044
E-mail sales@arcadiapublishing.com
For customer service and orders:
Toll-Free 1-888-313-2665

Visit us on the Internet at www.arcadiapublishing.com

*To my mom, Helen O. Larson, who, when first
married, made her home in Colvintown*

CONTENTS

Acknowledgments   6

Introduction   7

1.   Anthony   9

2.   Arkwright and Harris   25

3.   Coventry Centre   31

4.   Greene   39

5.   Hopkins Hollow   57

6.   Quidnick   63

7.   Rice City and Vaughn Hollow   69

8.   Summit   83

9.   Tiogue, Spring Lake, and Maple Root   97

10.   Washington and Colvintown   109

ACKNOWLEDGMENTS

Many of the readers of my past five books have commented on how my mother's poetry seems to bring my books alive. My mom, Helen O. Larson, was born in 1910 and wrote her first poem when she was 12. Her poetry writing culminated with her 1,700th poem, written two days before she passed away, in her 95th year. The opportunity to sprinkle verses of her work throughout the pages is what drives me to continue to do research and create yet another book. Writing these books has become a passion to me. This history needs to be recorded before it is lost, as the older folks, with all of their knowledge of the past, are passing on. Once lost, it is gone forever.

The following people have been outstanding to work with in creating this book: Dean Bentley, Donald Carpenter, Brendan Harrington, Leisa Jorgensen, Henriette Koszela, Richard Siembab, Gail Mitchell Slezak, Peter Stevens, Dave Underwood, and Normand D. Wolf.

Numerous people from the following organizations were also instrumental in its making: Coventry Historical Society, Pawtuxet Valley Preservation and Historical Society, Western Rhode Island Civic and Historical Society, Nathanael Greene Homestead, Paine House, and the Mittie Arnold Memorial Library.

I would like to thank Charles Despres for pointing out to me why the athletic field on Knotty Oak Road was dedicated as Rice Field. Because of his exhaustive efforts, his dream came true on November 11, 1995 (see pages 22 and 23).

I wish to especially thank Donald Carpenter and Richard Siembab for spending time proofreading this book for historical correctness.

All of the aforementioned people have loaned me their collections, graced me with their knowledge, and enthusiastically followed my progress. Thanks go to all of you.

I want to express my deepest appreciation to Jenn Carnevale, who has proofread all of my previous Images of America books: *The Lost Villages of Scituate*, *The Scituate Reservoir*, *West Warwick*, *Foster*, *Pawtuxet Valley Villages: Hope to Natick to Washington*, and now *Coventry*. She also helps staff my table at events along with my daughter Ashlee Rae. Jenn, you are a great friend.

In conclusion, I thank the great team I work with at Arcadia Publishing: Lissie Cain, acquisitions editor, Jennifer Pratt, regional sales and marketing manager, and all the people behind the scenes who are so good at making the Images of America series the greatest.

Unless otherwise noted, all images are from Richard Siembab's extensive, personal, and valued collection of Coventry memorabilia.

INTRODUCTION

Coventry is a companion volume to the author's books *West Warwick* and *Pawtuxet Valley Villages: Hope to Natick to Washington* and completes the coverage of all 25 villages in the area. Although it touches upon Arkwright, Harris, Washington, Anthony, and Quidnick, *Coventry* concentrates on Coventry Centre, Greene, Hopkins Hollow, Rice City, and Summit. It also refers to the areas of Colvintown, Maple Root, Spring Lake, Tiogue, and Vaughn Hollow.

Coventry was originally part of Warwick, beginning when Samuel Gorton negotiated, for 11 associates, the Shawomet Land Purchase from Miantonomi, chief sachem of the Narragansett Indians, in 1643. By the 1700s, the citizens of the western portion of the purchase were tired of traveling two to three days round-trip to the village of Apponaug to do their own business with the town. Therefore, they voted to break away from Warwick. On August 21, 1741, the area west of what is now West Warwick (then still Warwick) was incorporated into the Township of Coventry. It was named for Coventry, a township in Warwickshire, England. After the split, Coventry became the largest township in Rhode Island, a distinction it still holds. In 1748, the 64.8-square-mile township had fewer than 800 inhabitants.

The Providence & Plainfield Railroad laid tracks through the western portion of Coventry, and, in 1854, built the small Coffin depot near Coffin Road. In 1856, the Hartford, Providence & Fishkill Railroad took over the line and built a larger depot. It was named Greene in honor of Gen. Nathanael Greene, the Revolutionary War hero who was second-in-command to George Washington. The railroad line would change hands many times until, in 1898, it became the New York, New Haven & Hartford Railroad. With rail stations in Coventry Centre, Summit, and Greene, the western area of Coventry began to thrive.

There were gristmills and sawmills in the area dating back to the 1700s. However, the railroad gave settlers and mill owners a faster way to get their goods to market and receive supplies in return. The railroad also brought a new industry: harvesting wood to supply the locomotives with fuel to fire up the engines.

Population growth shifted from Rice City, Vaughn Hollow, and Hopkins Hollow to Greene, Summit, and Coventry Centre. Washington, Anthony, Quidnick, and Harris already had a strong population base because of the many mills that had been built along the Pawtuxet River. By 1941, the population of Coventry had increased to almost 20,000.

Coventry has had many outstanding citizens—enough to fill a book. In fact, that is what Andrew D. Boisvert is currently doing. His book *Legendary Locals of Coventry*, part of a separate series by Arcadia Publishing, will be published soon.

Coventry's population is now over 35,000, making it the seventh-largest of the 39 cities and towns in Rhode Island. Today, the stagecoach lines and the railroad lines have all disappeared. The mills have moved to the South, and most villagers now commute to work. The one-room schoolhouses have been replaced with regional schools, and, now, instead of walking to school, the students ride a bus. Instead of lanterns to read by, a fireplace to keep warm, a washboard to do laundry, and a horse for transportation, locals can flip a switch for all the modern conveniences and then hop in an automobile and take a ride through the country.

Fans of the author's mother's poetry will not be disappointed, as she begins the story of Coventry by reminiscing about a little lamp shop she and her husband, Ivar, used to frequent. It was called the Candle Snuffer and was located in Maple Root (see page 107). The author has also sprinkled in new verses of Helen O. Larson's poems throughout the pages of this book.

"The Candle Snuffer"
by Helen O. Larson

There's a quaint little shop in Maple Root
Run by an aunt, a daughter, and her mom
And as soon as I go through the door
I can see a lot of yester-year charm.

It's a small cottage by the water
It's so warm and cozy inside
It sits on the shore of a lake
We stop there when we go for a ride

As I walk up the steps I can see
A candle snuffer hung on the door
As I open the door and enter
There's a carpet of red on the floor

There's a beautiful hanging lamp
Hanging just over head
With a beautiful hand painted globe
With a cluster of roses of red

And on each wall
Are plaques of brass
On a stand there sits
An antique lamp of glass

There's a bridge lamp by a chair
Of Vasline glass it's made
There's another beautiful lamp
With a cranberry glass shade

There's a little old lamp in the corner
With a price tag on it, I see
I can almost hear it say
Won't someone please buy me

There's a small brass stand in the corner
And on it is a lamp that is old
And to Mrs. Sodergren and Phyllis
These antiques are more precious than gold

There's a little bird house in the yard
Where little birds come every day
They nibble on the crumbs for awhile
Then they fly far away

The shop has newly been shingled
The shingles have a fresh coat of stain
And when I am leaving, I know
I will go back again

At the gate there's a sign "Candle Snuffer"
It's a very cute little sign
It's such a quaint little shop
It takes me way back in time

As I close the door of the lamp shop
And as I am driving away
I leave a little of my heart in the lamp shop
But I know I'll go back some day

One

ANTHONY

Gen. Nathanael Greene's statue has been welcoming visitors to the south entrance of the Rhode Island statehouse in Providence since 1931. Greene was second-in-command to George Washington during the Revolutionary War. He was born in Warwick in 1742 and died at Mulberry Grove Plantation, near Savannah, Georgia, in 1786. In 1902, he was reburied in the base of a monument erected in his honor in Savannah's Johnson Square. (Author's collection.)

Nathanael Greene was born in the Potowomot area of Warwick in 1742. In 1770, he moved to Greenville (later changed to Anthony) and took charge of his father's forge. His homestead was built that same year, high on a hill overlooking the Pawtuxet River and the family forge. The homestead (above) was designed with four rooms off central hallways on each floor. Two major chimneys provided a fireplace for each of the eight rooms. The family parlor is seen below. The two closets were originally passageways to another room and created a way for heat to circulate. (Both, author's collection.)

Catharine Littlefield Greene's kitchen is seen above, well stocked with cooking utensils. The kitchen fireplace provided all the necessary compartments to cook a breakfast or full-scale dinner and keep it warm in the side-warming oven. The dining room, shown below, was across the hall. The window shutters, folded back during the day, were closed at night and helped keep the cold out during the long, cold New England winters. The homestead was purchased on June 30, 1919, by four members of the Kent County Chapter of the Rhode Island Sons of the American Revolution—Henry Greene Jackson, Herbert M. Clarke, Dr. Frank B. Smith, and Dr. Benjamin Franklin Tefft. After the home was restored, the Nathanael Greene Homestead Association opened it to the public in 1924. (Both, author's collection.)

William and Richard Anthony, along with others, built the first Coventry Manufacturing Company mill in 1806. The original mill store, pictured above, was built in 1807. It burned down on January 18, 1887, and was replaced by the building pictured on the cover of *Pawtuxet Valley Villages* and on page 106 of that book. It is also seen below, as the fourth building from the left in the distance. In the foreground, Ethel May Nicholas smiles for the camera on a cold winter day. She married Jesse Johnson of Anthony. (Below, Pawtuxet Valley Preservation and Historical Society.)

This is an aerial view of the Anthony mill complex. The small building to the left was the mill office. The building behind it replaced the original 1806 mill, which was only 125 feet long. The next building, constructed in 1810, was later converted to a warehouse. The five-story mill in the center was built in 1874 with an impressive tower in front. The mill on the right, beside the river, was built in 1910. A passageway over the tailrace connected the two mills. (Frederick Curtis.)

These three ladies wait for the train at the Anthony depot. They are, from left to right, Blanch Levesque, of New Haven, Connecticut, and her cousins Martha Levesque Rock and Bernadette Levesque Lesniak. The porch on the back of the Anthony Athletic Association building, on Washington Street, can be seen across the Pawtuxet River.

Searles Capwell was born in West Greenwich on April 8, 1838. He married Susan Greene in 1856 and they later moved to Anthony. She passed away on March 19, 1907. He then married Florence Briggs on June 23, 1908. Seen here in 1908 are, from left to right, (seated) Searles Capwell, Florence Briggs Capwell, her sister Ida Briggs Nicholas, and Josephine Tuckerman; (standing) Nina and Ethel Nicholas, the only children of Ambrose and Ida Nicholas. (Pawtuxet Valley Preservation and Historical Society.)

This 1907 postcard shows the impressive house Searles and Susan Capwell built at 681 Washington Street (now Main Street) in Anthony. The house still stands today. In 1906, the Capwells celebrated their 50th wedding anniversary with family and friends. She died the next year, and he died suddenly in 1916 after remarrying.

This postcard view shows the Searles Capwell Lumber Company in the early 1900s. Capwell was a large landowner in both West Greenwich and Coventry. Instead of clear-cutting his land, he used the process of selective cutting. After his death in 1916, the company fell apart.

This is a receipt from the Searles Capwell Lumber Company dated November 15, 1910. At the time, nails cost 3 1/2¢ a pound; wood shingles, $4 a bundle; and pine lumber, 29¢ a foot. The receipt also advertises that the business carries Lowe Bros. Standard Liquid Paints. (Charles Despres.)

This portrait of the Read family shows, from left to right, Herman Bryon Read (born February 17, 1878), Byron Read (born 1845), Charles Sheldon Read (born November 23, 1879), and Julia Ann Pinckney Read. The Reads were married in 1870.

Byron Read purchased the Oliver Matteson estate in 1887. He moved the existing house to Mapledale Avenue and built the house below. Frank Gorton, who was an embalmer for Read's son Herman and married into the family, later opened his own funeral parlor in the Byron Read mansion. It is still in business today at 721 Washington Street as the Gorton-Menard Funeral Home.

Byron Read had this 40-foot-by-100-foot, three-story (plus a basement) building constructed in 1882. At the time, it was the largest building in Coventry. In 1914, he built the small stone-block building to the left to house his hearses, which are proudly displayed out front in this photograph. (Donald Carpenter.)

ANTHONY, R. I., April 5 1937

M Est. Ambrose H. Nicholas

Greene, R.I.

IN ACCOUNT WITH

BYRON READ CO.

FUNERAL DIRECTORS

PHONE, VALLEY 124-M
OR VALLEY 808-W

MAIL ADDRESS
702 WASHINGTON STREET
WEST WARWICK, R. I.

FUNERAL EXPENSES OF Ambrose H. Nicholas

Burial case, Outside box, use of equipment, preparing body and services.	$475.00
Opening & closing grave	30.00
	$505.00

This is a receipt from the Byron Read Company, funeral directors, for the burial of Ambrose H. Nicholas, dated April 30, 1937. The cost of $505 included the burial case, outside box, use of equipment, preparing the body, and services. It also included opening and closing the grave. The receipt is signed by Frank R. Gorton, an employee. (Pawtuxet Valley Preservation and Historical Society.)

This portrait of Dr. Benjamin Tefft Jr. was taken in 1910 when he was 35. He was born in Pontiac, Warwick, on May 20, 1875. He completed grammar school in Arctic and was a member of the first class to graduate from Cranston High School in 1894. Tefft graduated with his medical degree from the University of Maryland on May 13, 1905, and opened his practice in Arctic in January 1909. (Western Rhode Island Civic and Historical Society.)

Dr. Benjamin Tefft Jr. married Mary Maria Matteson on August 5, 1903. She was the daughter of Dr. John and Julia Matteson of Anthony. The Teffts had one daughter, Hope Allen, born on August 9, 1909. This photograph was also taken in 1910. (Western Rhode Island Civic and Historical Society.)

This postcard of the Dr. Benjamin Tefft Jr. homestead, at 712 Washington Street, was mailed on June 3, 1908. It was across from Gorton's Funeral Home. The sender, Florence E. Briggs, wrote on the reverse, "Sent refrigerator about noon yesterday by electric freight." She signed it "F.E.B."

This 50-gallon soda and acid chemical fire truck was hand-drawn by the overseers of the mill. Chief Elmer A. Capwell is seen here standing on the extreme left. This wagon was bought by the Coventry Fire Company about 1912 and remained the only piece of fire equipment in Coventry until 1916, when the Coventry Fire District was organized. It was used in the 1916 Odd Fellows hall fire, seen on page 113 of *Pawtuxet Valley Villages*. (Anthony Fire Company.)

The following excerpt is from "The History of the Knotty Oak," as written in the 1936 Coventry High School yearbook: "In 1840 a group of worshipful people built a church not far away and although legally named the Coventry Central Six Principles Baptist Meeting House, it was soon called Knotty Oak Church." It also includes this poem: "When to a sleeping acorn/Mother Nature spoke/The little seed at once arose/And grew to be a famous oak." (Coventry Historical Society.)

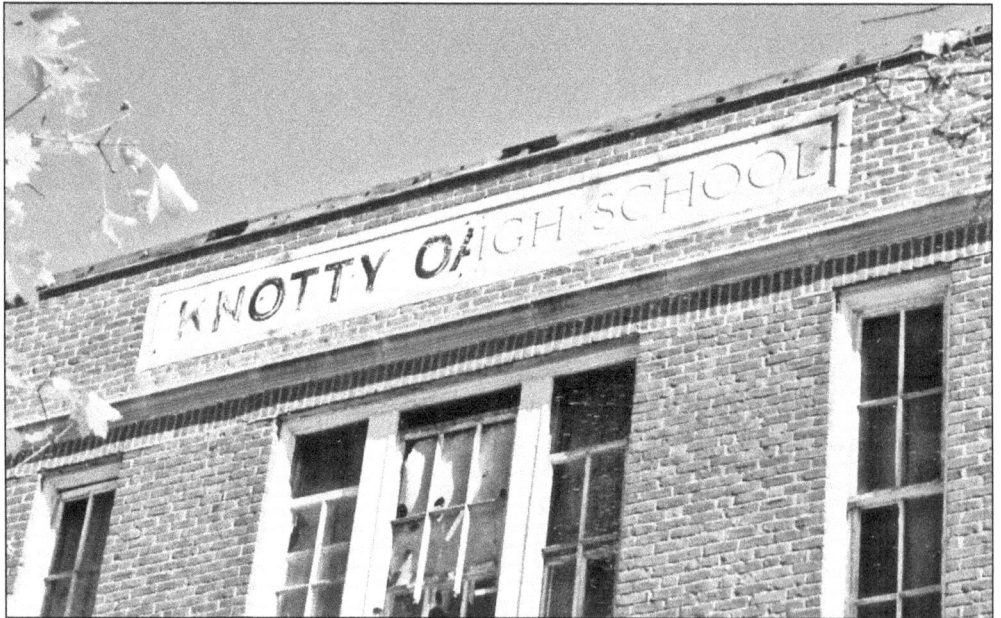

The new Coventry High School, on Knotty Oak Road, was dedicated on October 26, 1934. It was renamed Knotty Oak School and used as an elementary school after a new high school was constructed in 1958. Portions of both names the school was known by became visible when this photograph was taken during the building's demolition on November 1, 1993. (Joan Jervais.)

THE
KNOTTY OAK

C. H. S.
1936

This is the cover the 32 members of the graduating class of 1936 chose for their yearbook. The "History of the Knotty Oak" continues: "Unlike most oak trees this one did not grow to be lofty and majestic but, due to powerful forces of wind, storm, and cold, became a gnarled and knotty oak. A highway was to be constructed and the tree in the way must be removed. In the fall of 1905, the Knotty Oak, was cut down. Thus the history of the Knotty Oak, which covered over two hundred years, was ended. The tree is dead but its name lives on in this book. Is it not fitting that we of the Coventry High School should name our Year Book after this tree, and in so doing, hope that it, too, might catch some of the spirit of the Knotty Oak." (Coventry Historical Society.)

IN GRATEFUL MEMORY OF

Wilson Albert Rice

WHO DIED IN THE SERVICE OF HIS COUNTRY AT

Pearl Harbor, T. H., attached U.S.S. Curtiss, 7 December 1941

HE STANDS IN THE UNBROKEN LINE OF PATRIOTS WHO HAVE DARED TO DIE

THAT FREEDOM MIGHT LIVE, AND GROW, AND INCREASE ITS BLESSINGS.

FREEDOM LIVES, AND THROUGH IT, HE LIVES—

IN A WAY THAT HUMBLES THE UNDERTAKINGS OF MOST MEN

Franklin D Roosevelt

PRESIDENT OF THE UNITED STATES OF AMERICA

In the early 1940s, the Coventry School Committee voted to name the athletic field behind the original high school Wilson Rice Field to honor the first young man from the Pawtuxet Valley to die in World War II. Rice lost his life aboard the USS *Curtis* during the Japanese attack on Pearl Harbor on December 7, 1941. This notification was signed by Pres. Franklin D. Roosevelt. (Coventry Historical Society.)

IN GRATEFUL MEMORY OF

Private Donald S. Rice

WHO DIED IN THE SERVICE OF HIS COUNTRY

in the European Area, April 18, 1945.

HE STANDS IN THE UNBROKEN LINE OF PATRIOTS WHO HAVE DARED TO DIE

THAT FREEDOM MIGHT LIVE, AND GROW, AND INCREASE ITS BLESSINGS

FREEDOM LIVES, AND THROUGH IT, HE LIVES—

IN A WAY THAT HUMBLES THE UNDERTAKINGS OF MOST MEN

Harry Truman

PRESIDENT OF THE UNITED STATES OF AMERICA

Before Wilson Rice Field was completed, the Rice family suffered another loss when Wilson's brother Donald S. Rice, a private in the Army, was killed in action in Germany on April 18, 1945. The name to be given to the field was then changed to Rice Memorial Field to honor both brothers. This notification, sent to his parents, was signed by Pres. Harry S. Truman. (Coventry Historical Society.)

Charles Despres had a dream to place a monument so people would know why the athletic field on Knotty Oak Road was called Rice Field. His dream was fulfilled on Saturday, November 11, 1995, at 2:00 p.m., when the monument was uncovered. He felt it was appropriate for the ceremony to be held on Veteran's Day in the 50th anniversary year of the end of World War II. (Charles Despres.)

Charles Despres is seen here on June 12, 2012, telling the author the story of the two brothers from Coventry who lost their lives in World War II. He stands proudly in front of the monument dedicating the field to Wilson and Donald Rice. The funds for the monument were provided by the Coventry Credit Union, and Guy Lefebvre provided the foundation. (Author's collection.)

Eddie Zack began his singing career at age 16 with his brother Richie, who was later known as Cousin Richie. The photograph shows the Texas Dollies performing at Manchester Hall in Eddie Zack's Cowboy Cavalcade in the 1950s. They are, from left to right, Patsy, Mickey, Shirley, and Betty. Eddie Zack and the Hayloft Jamboree celebrated 60 years in country music in January 1999. He was inducted into the Rockabilly Hall of Fame on June 1, 1999.

This photograph shows Manchester Hall, at 585 Washington Street, in 2012. It is still the headquarters of Manchester Lodge No. 12 of the Free and Accepted Masons. (Author's collection.)

Two

ARKWRIGHT AND HARRIS

This photograph, taken from the roof of the Arkwright mill, shows the dam and bridge in 1968. In the 1700s, the area was known as Remington's Run, in honor of the Remington family. It later became Burlingame's Mills. In 1809, James DeWolf, Dr. Caleb Fiske, Fiske's son Philip, and Asher Robbins formed the Arkwright Manufacturing Company. They then named the village Arkwright, in honor of the English inventor Richard Arkwright. (Donald Carpenter.)

The beautiful postcard view above shows the Harris mill, which was built in 1851 by Elisha Harris. This was Harris's second mill; he built one in 1822 on the opposite side of the road, which was torn down in 1902. Below is a photograph of the mill office of the first mill, on Main Street opposite the home of Harris's brother David's house. The following verse is from "Buildings That Were Destroyed" by Helen O. Larson: "The mill was destroyed/Where my father worked each day/Oh! The pain and heartache/To see it torn down and carried away." (Above, Pawtuxet Valley Preservation and Historical Society; below, Donald Carpenter.)

This photograph of David Harris's house is dated October 1914. The house still stands today at 590 Main Street, on the corner of Harris Street. The existing Harris mill complex is in the right background.

This drawing is from the cover of a binder holding the newspaper report regarding the fire that destroyed Harris Heights School on January 22, 1971. The school was never rebuilt. The author attended the fourth-grade class at Harris Heights for nine long weeks. (Coventry Historical Society.)

Harris Heights School
Coventry, Rhode Island
1845 - - - 1971

Harris Heights School was built in 1845 and burned down in 1971. It is seen above in 1900 and can also be seen in *Pawtuxet Valley Villages* on page 51. The 1899 graduates are seen below. They are, from left to right, (first row) Frank Duffy, Patrick Barry, Howard Walker, and Eddie Cunningham; (second row) Katie Love, Marie Dennegan, Grace Vickery, Marie Thornton, Lizzie Forrest, and Kate O'Niel; (third row) Hattie Sherman, Annie Whitford, Edna Round, Eugenie Whitford, Annie Johnson, Hattie Sweet, Lizzie Tweedly, and Mabel Taylor. (Above, Pawtuxet Valley Preservation and Historical Society.)

This class picture of Harris Heights School students was taken in 1910. It appears that classes were getting larger. Earl Handy (fourth row, second from left) is the only student identified. (Donald Carpenter.)

Taken Early 1940's L to R
Elizabeth Murnigham   Gr 3-4
Lucy Potter   Gr 5-6
Elsie Cowan   Gr 7-8
Ada Sykes   Gr 1-2

Seen here are the four teachers who taught at Harris Heights in the 1940s. They are, from left to right, Elizabeth Murnigham, grades three and four; Lucy Potter, grades five and six; Elsie Cowan, grades seven and eight; and Ada Sykes, grades one and two. Cowan taught at the school for 32 years and was also the principal. Sykes was a teacher there for 36 years. (Coventry Historical Society.)

This 1908 photograph shows three generations of the Hudson family at 50 Mumford Street in Harris. The oldest two people identified are J. Ellery Hudson and his wife, Eliza J. Hudson, in the middle of the second row. (Donald Carpenter.)

The Wheelock family is seen here in Harris in 1905. They are, from left to right, Martha Brayton Wheelock, her husband, Lloyd; Mary Wheelock Hawkins; Nina Wheelock; Jesse Wheelock Knight; Charles Herman Wheelock; Anieanette Crandall Wheelock (rear); Minnie Wiley; her sister Susie Wiley Wheelock; and Susie's husband, Frank. (Donald Carpenter.)

Three

COVENTRY CENTRE

This postcard, mailed in July 1909, shows the lower portion of Coventry Centre. The lower mill, seen here, was built in 1859 and manufactured cotton yarn. In 1879, a town house was built here, and the town government was moved from Potterville. However, in 1881, it was moved again to Washington, where it has remained.

The early-1900s postcard above shows the upper mill in Coventry Centre, where cloth was manufactured. The view looks north on Phillips Hill Road to Route 117. Larry Arnold built the first mill on this site in 1809, but it burned down. It was rebuilt in 1845 and then sold to Pardon S. Peckham. In 1866, after Thomas C. and John G. Peckham joined the firm, a new corporation was formed: Peckham Manufacturing Company. The chimney to the left of the mill above is the same one seen below with a house attached to it in 2012. (Below, author's collection.)

Above is another view of the Pardon S. Peckham Manufacturing Company's upper mill and the railroad passing through. The water tower of the lower mill is in the upper left corner. The Hartford, Providence & Fishkill Railroad ran on this line from 1849 until 1878, when it became the New York & New England Railroad. It ran under that name until 1895, when it became the New England Railroad for three years. By 1898, it was the New York, New Haven & Hartford Railroad. The last train passed through this area in 1966. The ticket below is dated April 27, 1889. (Both, Donald Carpenter.)

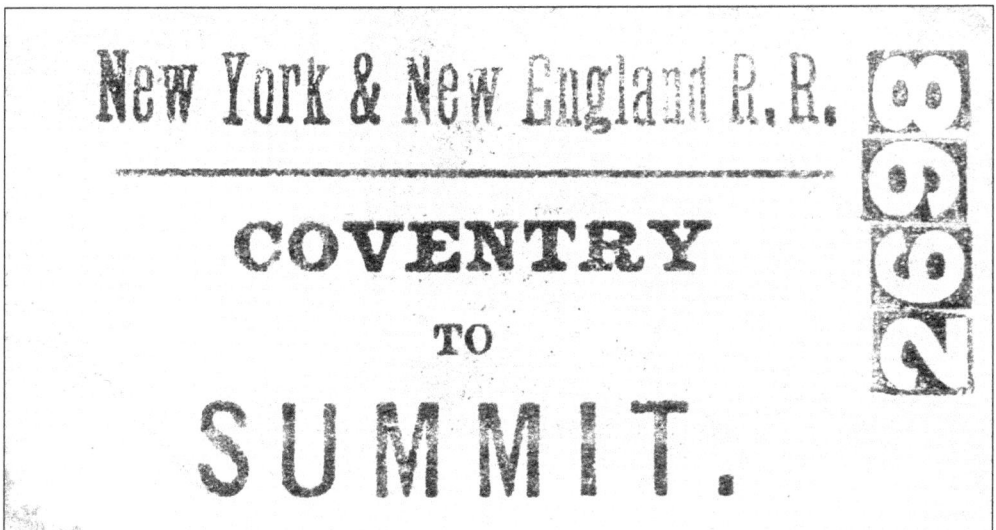

New York & New England R.R.

2698

COVENTRY

TO

SUMMIT.

The postcard above shows Harry Bentley's general store, on the corner of Flat River and Phillips Hill Roads. Bentley also maintained the post office for Coventry Centre residents. His wife, Phoebe, was the postmistress. The second and third floors of the building were used as a boardinghouse for mill workers. Note the fountain in the square beside the two men, which was there for the convenience of thirsty horses. The three duplexes are still in use today. The lower mill and the water tower are seen below. The additions to the left were built in 1864. (Above, Coventry Historical Society; below, Pawtuxet Valley Preservation and Historical Society.)

William Holt is seen above in the early 1900s with his uncomplicated but well-built delivery truck for the Rhode Island Processing Company. The side of the truck advertises that the company offers services as "Mercerizers, Bleachers, Dyers & Converters." In his right hand, he holds the tip of a "Providence" banner so it can be seen by the camera. The postcard below shows a good view of the lower mill, the 1864 addition, and the water tower. The postcard was given to customers and prospective customers as an advertising tool. (Both, Donald Carpenter.)

COMPLIMENTS OF

THE HOME OF THE RHODE ISLAND PROCESSING CO.

W. R. GILLESPIE,
Gen'l Mgr.

COVENTRY, R. I.

This mission church was originally founded as Christ Church over 100 years ago. In 2010, it merged with St. Matthias Church and was renamed St. Francis Episcopal Church. The structure above was built in 1918 on Peckham Lane and features a protected side entrance on the right and a belfry on the gable end in front. Below, vicar Beth Sherman, in white, prepares for Sunday service. Note the beautifully beamed ceiling. (Above, author's collection; below, Donald Carpenter.)

This postcard shows Coventry Centre School sitting proudly on top of a hill. It was very large for the time period, with five bays on the side. It had the standard separate entrances for girls and boys in the front, along with the belfry, which announced the beginning of classes for the students.

The first bridge built for the Hartford, Providence & Fishkill Railroad was replaced by this steel-beam bridge in 1910 for the New York, New Haven & Hartford Railroad. It is slated to be part of the East Coast Greenway Alliance, whose goal is to create a 3,000-mile off-road trail connecting cities from Canada to Key West, Florida. The trail is 25-percent complete. This postcard view was taken in the mid-1970s when Flat River Road (Route 117) was being reconstructed.

The postcard above of the Coventry Centre railroad station was mailed in 1914. The station was built in 1856, and the line was finally abandoned exactly 100 years later. The Waterman Tavern is seen below in 1900. John Waterman built the tavern about 1747 and it was used for town meetings in the early days. Stagecoaches stopped there as late as 1856, when railroad travel took over. A plaque mounted to a boulder in the front yard reads, "Used as headquarters for the French Troops on their march to and from Yorktown 1781–1782 Maj. Gen. Nathanael Greene, Gen. Lafayette, and Gen. Rochambeau." It is listed in the National Register of Historic Places. (Above, Donald Carpenter; below, Pawtuxet Valley Preservation and Historical Society.)

Four

GREENE

The Providence, Hartford & Fishkill Railroad built a depot in this wilderness area in the 1850s. The railroad decided to name it Greene in honor of Gen. Nathanael Greene. The view in this 1905 postcard of Greene looks east on Hopkins Hollow Road. The Greene Library (page 52) now occupies the empty lot on the left.

This postcard view shows Hopkins Hollow Road on the left, headed towards Summit. On the right is the Greene Depot. A sign on the depot advertises Western Union Telegraph service inside. A Ward's Tip-Top Bread sign is leaning against the tree. (David Underwood.)

This postcard view shows engine 1697 patiently waiting on the main line track while passengers board. The middle, or passing, track went to the east end of Benefit Street. On the house track on the right, a man loads lumber into a New York, New Haven & Hartford boxcar. The Masonic hall is behind the depot.

In this postcard mailed on October 29, 1913, the view looking south is from beside the depot on Hopkins Hollow Road. The boxcar on the right is on the house track by the storage shed.

A well-dressed crowd waits at the second Greene depot, built in 1856. It replaced the small makeshift station built in 1854. Locomotive 1546 is about to roll to a stop on the main line track so passengers can board.

The Nicholas homestead, built in 1813, is seen above in 1909. At one time, the farm was so large that it spread into Connecticut, and it even had its own school, the Nicholas District School. Pictured, from left to right, are Ethel May Nicholas, "Grandma" Mary Briggs, Ambrose Nicholas, unidentified, Ida Briggs Nicholas, unidentified, "Grandpa" Caleb Ray Nicholas, and Nina B. Nicholas. Seen at left in their Sunday best in 1895 are, from left to right, Ida Briggs Nicholas, Nina B. Nicholas (in baby carriage), Florence E. Briggs, and Ethel May Nicholas. (Both, Pawtuxet Valley Preservation and Historical Society.)

A 15-year-old Nina B. Nicholas is seen here at the Nicholas homestead on Nicholas Road. She is all dressed up and celebrating her graduation from the ninth grade in June 1910. (Pawtuxet Valley Preservation and Historical Society.)

Coventry Public Schools.

Report of *Nina Nicholas*

Greene School, Grade IX

19*09* — 19 *10*	Oct. 31	Dec. 31	Feb. 28	Apr. 30	June 30
Algebra	G	G	E	E	E
Arithmetic	E	E	E	G	E
Drawing	E	E		E	E
Geography and Nature	E	E	C	E	E
History	G	G	E	G+	E
Language	H	H	H	G	E
Music	G	G		G	G
Penmanship	E	E		E	E
Physiology and Hygiene	G	E	E	E	E
Reading and Literature	G	G	G	G	G
Spelling	G	E	E		E
Number Times Absent	1	5	0	0	0
Number Times Tardy	0	3	0	0	0
Number Times Dismissed	0	0	0	0	0
Deportment	E	E	H	E	E
Effort	G	E	H	E	E

M. E. McManus TEACHER.
Elizabeth F. Mc Greevy.

Nina B. Nicholas's report card for the ninth grade, in June 1910, is seen here. She ended the year with all Es (excellent) except in music, reading, and literature, in which she received Gs (good). Her teachers were M.E. McManus and Elizabeth F. McGreevy. On the back of the report card, the "Signature of Parent" for each quarter was signed by her father Ambrose H. Nicholas, who was elected to the state senate in 1912. (Pawtuxet Valley Preservation and Historical Society.)

Curnel S. Brown moved from West Greenwich in 1882 and converted a grain building into the house pictured, constructing an ell addition. He became postmaster in 1885 and held the position for 27 years. He also boarded horses in the barn at the rear. He advertised that boarding a horse cost 25¢ a day if he fed them and 15¢ if he did not. This was the location of the Greene post office when this postcard was mailed on October 24, 1906.

Lorin Spencer and Harriet Burlingame are seen here on September 3, 1921. Spencer married Mary Burlingame, and Mary's brother William married Harriet. (David Underwood.)

Margaret Thomas and Mittie Arnold operated Greene Herb Gardens on the Arnold Estate (page 51) from the 1950s to the 1970s. They grew, dried, and packaged herbs for shipment. Below is a sampler box of three bags, each with eight of the company's herbs. The back of the box reads, "What goes with what? Here are 24 bags of green(e) herbs for 24 sample seasonings." The following verse is from "The Garden," written by Helen O. Larson when she was 77: "As I walk through the garden, I hear a Robin sing/Then I glance at my finger/And see your golden ring." The postcard above was distributed at the Golden Garden Spring Flower Show, at the Mechanics Building in Boston on March 15–21, 1953.

HERB SAMPLER

GREENE HERB GARDENS, GREENE, R.I.

This Herb Sampler contains 3 bags each of:–
Basil   Marjoram
Celery   Parsley
Kale   Poultry Seasoning
Salad Herbs   Meat Seasoning
Combined Net Weight:– Approx. 1 oz.

The postcard above shows the Greene schoolhouse, built in 1872, which had a small room for the very young students and a large room for all of the others. It had the standard separate entrances for boys and girls in front, as well as a flagpole. The 1909 class includes, from left to right, (first row) John Hoover, Gladys Lemis, Myrtle Sherman, Esther Perkins, Bessie Mason, Ethel Hoover, Earl Capwell, and Harold Capwell; (second row) Harold Mason, Everett Potter, Nina B. Nicholas (teacher), Mary E. McManus, Elsie Mason, and Walter Brown. (Above, David Underwood.)

The people of the village of Greene attended Rice City Christian Baptist Church from 1857 until 1870, when Whipple V. and Robie Phillips, George W. and Lois Rider, and Esek and Emeline Griffith withdrew from the Rice City church and formed Greene Methodist Church. In 1873, this 40-foot-by-80-foot building was constructed. For many years, Maxwell Mays (page 94) was the preacher. This photograph was taken in July 2012. (Author's collection.)

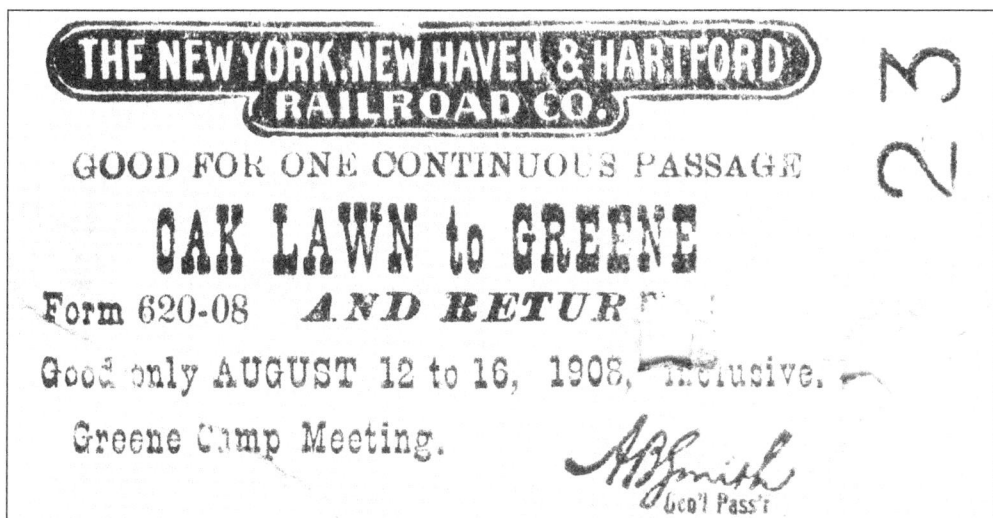

This round-trip ticket took its owner from Oak Lawn, Warwick, directly to Greene, Coventry, aboard the New York, New Haven & Hartford Railroad. It was only good during the annual Greene camp meeting, held August 12–16, 1908. (David Underwood.)

The first Advent Christian camp meeting was held in 1874 in a tent at Rider's Corner. For the next five years, the Advents held the meetings in Coventry Centre. The meetings grew to last for several days, culminating with "Big Sunday." In 1880, the group bought 50 acres, pictured above, in Greene from Squire G. Wood and built a large boardinghouse. The meetings were then held for 10 days in a large tent. Many attendees would set up their own tent to stay the whole 10 days. In later years, some families decided to build their own cabins, as the family below did.

The tabernacle (above), a large, open-sided building, was built in 1880. Preaching began at the crack of dawn and extended well into the evening. It started on Friday and lasted for 10 days, ending with Big Sunday. For several years, thousands attended, coming from miles around. The New England Railroad and later the New Haven Railroad ran trains with reduced fares during the meetings. On Big Sunday, they would have 10 to 15 cars full of attendees. By 1929, electric lights had been added and all the buildings had been repaired. However, because attendance had gone down, the event was reduced to five days. The dining hall is seen below in the 1940s.

Laboratory workers at the Arnold Chemical Factory enjoy a break in the sunshine. They are, from left to right, (first row) Jack Morrison, Brian ?, Lee Burdick, John Aldrich, Joseph McCabe, Nelson Capwell, and David Fry. The four workers in the rear are unidentified.

This postcard also shows workers at the Arnolds Chemical Factory. The only men identified are Nelson Capwell (kneeling on left), Ed Arnold (standing behind him), William House (standing, third from left), Earl Capwell (kneeling on right), and George Chase (behind him).

The 1913 postcard above shows the back of the Arnold's farm. Edward E. Arnold was born on December 17, 1853, in this farmhouse his father, Nathaniel, owned. On January 3, 1889, he married Mittie Hodges of Peoria, Illinois. They had six children, one of whom was named Mittie after her mother. The farmhouse is seen at right in a Christmas card sent out by Mittie Arnold. The following verse is from "Christmas" by Helen O. Larson: "In every window of the houses in the villages/There's a Christmas tree sparkling with lights/You can see them all decorated/As you slowly ride by at night/You can hear the carolers singing/As they stand out in the snow/How sweetly their voices echo/Singing all the hymns they know."

Christmas Greetings
Mittie Arnold

Arnold Home

Mittie Arnold started the Greene Library in 1923. The one-and-a-half-story building was constructed in 1929. Arnold, known for her herb gardens (page 45) bequeathed $100,000 to be kept in a trust fund to keep the building going. She passed away on January 12, 1972, and, in 1973, the library was dedicated in her memory as the Mittie Arnold Memorial Library. In 2010, it became a branch of the Coventry Library. The Greene Library Association retains ownership of the building. The library's interior is seen below in the 1930s. Abbie Underwood spent 15 years as librarian here after leaving the librarian position at Western Coventry Elementary School. She retired, again, at the age of 80 in 1983. (Below, Pawtuxet Valley Preservation and Historical Society.)

Abbie M. Underwood is seen here with her granddaughter Robin Briggs Petrarca (left) and her daughter Frances Briggs in 2000. Her late husband, Lester Underwood, was the chief of the Western Coventry Fire Department. She passed away in 2003 at the age of 99. (David Underwood.)

Abbie Underwood taught in Foster and Coventry Centre. She is seen here with her first- and second-graders in 1958 at Western Coventry Elementary School, where she taught for 30 years before taking the position of school librarian for another eight years. (Coventry Historical Society.)

Abiel T. Sampson bought a cranberry bog three miles south of Greene from the Town of Coventry in 1862 at public auction. He named it the American Cranberry Company. During the nearly 30 years he owned the bogs, the cranberries were always picked by hand. Above, Raymond J. Siembab (left) and Ralph Theroux show off the first mechanized cranberry picker in 1950. Theroux was the foreman of the bog for 45 years, retiring at age 76.

After the death of Abiel Sampson, the bogs passed through many owners, went through foreclosure, and were then bought by a Boston company. Under new ownership as Coventry Cranberry Company and after many improvements, the business thrived. Here, Allan Moore leads a crew in the bogs in the late 1940s. (David Underwood.)

The original barn, built in 1867, burned down in the late 1800s. It was replaced with the one pictured, which was the same size but had an ell added in front in 1936. This is where the cranberries are still processed before they are shipped to Ocean Spray. In the early 1970s, the local cranberry company became and remains the Greene Company.

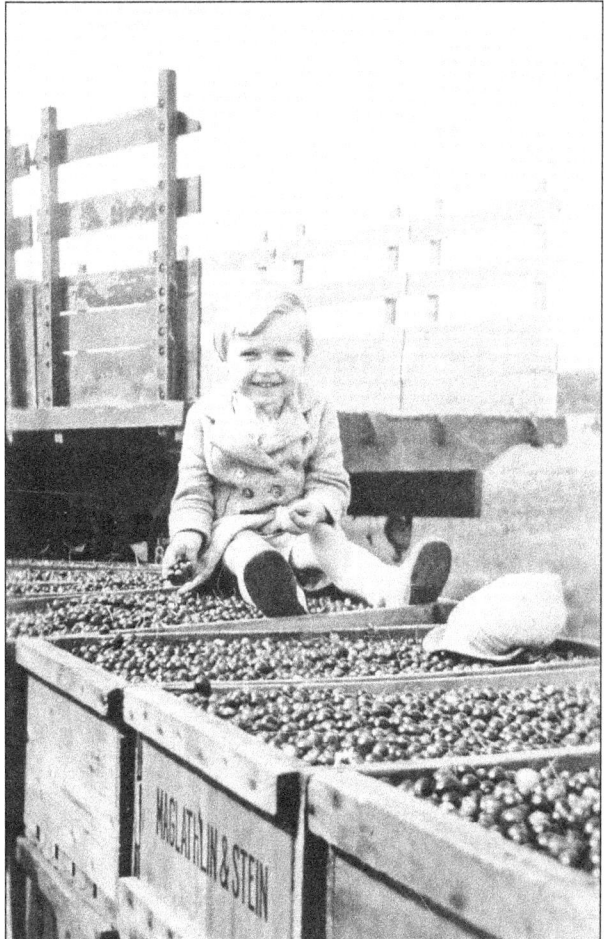

Three-year-old M. Lorraine Theroux Lozier enjoys a ride on crates of cranberries on an autumn day in 1940. She and her family lived on the bog property for about eight years. She remembers, "I used to sit in the truck—no seat belts then—beside my dad, Ralph Theroux, to deliver the load to the Ocean Spray Company in Middleboro, Massachusetts." (Henriette Koszela.)

In 1854, the Providence & Plainfield Railroad built track through an area of land owned by the Coffin family. The railroad built a small station and named it Coffin depot. In 1856, the Hartford, Providence & Fishkill Railroad took over the line and changed the name of the depot to Greene in honor of Gen. Nathanael Greene. The photograph at left shows station agent Roscoe Potter (left) and signalman Charles McCarthy on the day the station closed, April 30, 1954. The photograph below shows the excursion train, the last train to pass through Greene, in October 1966. The original Tanner house was built in 1890. When it burned, Tanner's widow built the one seen below to the left of the train tracks. (Both, David Underwood.)

Five

HOPKINS HOLLOW

The note on the side of this 1906 postcard reads, "Road leading from church down through Hopkins Hollow." Capt. Richard Rice built the first house here in the mid-1700s. He then constructed a sawmill and a gristmill, and the area became known as Rice's Mills. The name was changed to Hopkins Hollow after Jeremiah Hopkins and his son Samuel moved here and built a mill and blacksmith shop in 1825.

Above, a young Carrie Jordan, along with her horse Bess and her trusty dog, is out for a ride in her carriage with the top down. She later wed John H. Trenn, and they were married until he passed away in 1937. At left, Carrie Jordan Trenn and her dog stop again for the camera, this time in the mid-1900s. In 1941, when she was 62, she took on the job of transporting the local children to school and back home, which she did for 12 years. With double sessions, she was driving 20,000 miles a year. She favored Buicks and was a loyal customer of Main Street Buick in East Greenwich. She passed away in 1979 at the age of 100. (Both, Brendan Harrington.)

The photograph above was taken at the 100th anniversary of the Jordan family homestead, on Hopkins Hollow Road, in 1900. The only person identified in the group is Carrie Jordan Trenn, who is standing to the left of the lady seated with her hands in her lap. The following verse is from "Carrie Was Her Name" by Helen O. Larson: "If an angel ever came to earth/Carrie was that one/ And if there is a place called Heaven/There was a place reserved there when her work was done." The original caption of the photograph below states that "Grandma Jordan" was "blind for 20 years." The plaque above the doors reads, "The Lord Is My Shepherd." (Both, Brendan Harrington.)

Taken July-6-1906-

Hopkins Hollow Meeting-house.

Christian Baptist Church. *F.E.B.*

The Hopkins Hollow meetinghouse, seen above in 1906, was built in 1862. Its leader, Rev. George H. Holcomb, died while clearing the stairs of snow in the 1930s. Florence E. Briggs, "F.E.B.," was the sender of this postcard. Below is a view of the church, the school, and the cemetery, which was organized in 1840, predating the church. The school (page 62) is no longer, but the church was saved. The following verse is from "I Write the Words He Gives Me," which was written by Helen O. Larson at age 90: "Without His guidance, and telling me what to say/To write beautiful poems, I could do it no way/Yes, I'll go on writing, as long as I can see/And as long as I can hold a pen, I'll write the words He gives to me."

The Hopkins Hollow Cemetery, seen above in 2012, was organized 22 years before the congregation built the meetinghouse on the opposite page. Below, the headstone on the left reads, "William Capwell, died November 23, 1878 in the 79th year of his age, Gone but not Forgotten." The stone on the right reads, "Nancy Capwell, wife of William Capwell, Died March 2, 1881 in the 83rd year of her age, Asleep in Jesus." The following is from "A Place Called Heaven" by Helen O. Larson: "I know there is a Heaven, for I was there one night/I walked a golden street, and saw a brilliant light/Then I woke in the morning, and found it was only a dream/But as long as I live, I'll remember the beautiful mansions I have seen." (Both, author's collection.)

July 6 - 1906

Does this look familiar to you?
July 26 1906

F. E. B.

Our Old School House!

The original Hopkins Hollow school is seen in this 1906 postcard. Florence E. Briggs, "F.E.B.," posted this note to her friend: "Does this look familiar to you? Our old school house!" The school was built in the mid-1850s and replaced in 1872, when a larger school was constructed on Hopkins Hollow Road (page 46). It was located to the right of the Hopkins Hollow Church (see page 60). The photograph below was taken in February 2013 and shows the foundation of the school pictured above. (Below, author's collection.)

Six

QUIDNICK

Jimmie Rock proudly displays his 1936 Chevrolet pickup truck around 1950. It is parked in the National Market parking lot, on the corner of Washington Street and Bates Avenue. In the background is the rectory of Our Lady of Czenstochowa, also seen on page 100 of *Pawtuxet Valley Villages*. (Pawtuxet Valley Preservation and Historical Society.)

The Greene family purchased 94 acres of land in this area in 1740. Steven Taft bought a portion of it in 1823 and built a small mill. He named his village Taftville. The mill was then purchased by the A.W. Sprague Company in 1848. Later, when Horace Foster built this beautiful mill, he named the mill and the village Quidnick.

This postcard, mailed in March 1908, shows the massive abutment of the railroad bridge on the extreme right. It carried the Hartford, Providence & Fishkill Railroad over the south branch of the Pawtuxet River. Horace Foster built it, along with the Quidnick dam, in the foreground. The granite was from his Foster Ledge quarry in Coventry Centre. The Anthony mill is in the distance. A view of a train crossing the bridge can be seen on page 101 of *Pawtuxet Valley Villages*.

This building, at 487 Washington Street, was constructed in 1849 by Horace Foster as a company store for workers at the Quidnick mill. Moore's Motor Service began business in Lippitt, West Warwick, in the early 1920s, and then relocated here in 1927. It can also be seen on page 99 of *Pawtuxet Valley Villages*. (Donald Carpenter.)

This postcard view looks east as Washington Street leaves Anthony towards Quidnick. The Pawtuxet River is on the right, behind the fence. The trolley tracks in the road run parallel to the fence. Moore's Motors is around the next corner on the left.

This is a stunning postcard view of the Quidnick Grammar School. The two-story building was constructed in 1902. As usual, the girls' entrance was on the left and the boys' was on the right. The following verse is from "My School" by Helen O. Larson: "Oh! That dear old school house, that I loved so well/I miss it so much, more than words could tell."

The Only CAB Service Open 24 Hours A Day

VALLEY 0071-J

EMERGENCY
CALLS
GIVEN
IMMEDIATE
ATTENTION

Minute Man Cab

DIRECT SERVICE ANYWHERE

OFFICE & WAITING ROOM

110 WASHINGTON ST., (ARCTIC) WEST WARWICK, R. I.

REGGIE DiPRETE, Prop.

This is a photograph of a blotter the Minute Man Cab Company used for advertising. In schools in 1902, pupils used a pen dipped into an inkwell for writing. Then they would use a blotter to soak up any extra ink to avoid smudging. Residents of Quidnick who needed a cab knew to call "the only cab service open 24 hours a day." (Pawtuxet Valley Preservation and Historical Society.)

Included with this letter from Pres. Theodore Roosevelt on April 15, 1907, was the following note from William Loeb Jr., the secretary to the president: "My Dear Sir: I enclose a copy of the President's letter on Arbor Day to the children of the United States. This letter is being sent to the children thru the school officers of each State and Territory. If you can assist the President in reaching the children of your jurisdiction he will greatly appreciate your cooperation." (Coventry Historical Society.)

To the School Children of the United States:

Arbor Day (which means simply "Tree Day") is now observed in every State in our Union—and mainly in the schools. At various times from January to December, but chiefly in this month of April, you give a day or part of a day to special exercises and perhaps to actual tree planting, in recognition of the importance of trees to us as a Nation, and of what they yield in adornment, comfort, and useful products to the communities in which you live.

It is well that you should celebrate your Arbor Day thoughtfully, for within your lifetime the Nation's need of trees will become serious. We of an older generation can get along with what we have, though with growing hardship; but in your full manhood and womanhood you will want what nature once so bountifully supplied, and man so thoughtlessly destroyed; and because of that want you will reproach us, not for what we have used, but for what we have wasted.

For the nation as for the man or woman and the boy or girl, the road to success is the right use of what we have and the improvement of present opportunity. If you neglect to prepare yourselves now for the duties and responsibilities which will fall upon you later, if you do not learn the things which you will need to know when your school days are over, you will suffer the consequen-

---

ces. So any nation which in its youth lives only for the day, reaps without sowing, and consumes without husbanding, must expect the penalty of the prodigal, whose labor could with difficulty find him the bare means of life.

A people without children would face a hopeless future; a country without trees is almost as hopeless; forests which are so used that they can not renew themselves will soon vanish, and with them all their benefits. A true forest is not merely a storehouse full of wood, but, as it were, a factory of wood, and at the same time a reservoir of water. When you help to preserve our forests or to plant new ones you are acting the part of good citizens. The value of forestry deserves, therefore, to be taught in the schools, which aim to make good citizens of you. If your Arbor Day exercises help you to realize what benefits each one of you receives from the forests, and how by your assistance these benefits may continue, they will serve a good end.

THEODORE ROOSEVELT.

THE WHITE HOUSE,
        April 15, 1907.

Walter E. Ranger, the commissioner of public schools wrote back to the White House: "In response to your letter of the thirteenth of April, I have taken pleasure in arranging for the printing of 30,000 copies of the President's letter on Arbor Day for distribution among the school children and youth of Rhode Island. The distribution will be made in connection with that of our Arbor Day annual for 1907." (Coventry Historical Society.)

The old Tin Top Baptist Church in Quidnick is seen here. It got its name from its tin steeple. Originally framed in Providence, it was then rafted downriver to Apponaug and pulled by a team of horses to this location. Jacob Greene, a devout Quaker and the brother of Gen. Nathanael Greene, graciously donated the land the church sits on.

The plain interior of the Tin Top Baptist Church is seen here. Painted on the anchor in the balcony is the inscription "Hope Is In The Lord." The plaque below the clock reads "1808," the year the church was built. In later years, the church became the home of St. Mary's Parochial School.

Seven

RICE CITY AND
VAUGHN HOLLOW

Rice City schoolchildren pose for this photograph in 1913. They are, from left to right, (first row) Howard Kettle, unidentified, Frances Perry, Beatrice Bushee, and George Potter; (second row) unidentified, Helen Bushee, John Tew, unidentified, Wilmore Spaulding, and Helen Ridgeway; (third row) Abbie Fry, Charlotte Perry, Alton Kettle, Tom Philmore, and teacher Gertrude Briggs.

John Kettle (far left) is seen above with his workers in 1909. His sawmill was set up at the base of Carbuncle Hill. The photograph below, one of the oldest in this book, was taken in 1887. On the reverse side is written, "This is a picture of the little house on the Charles Vaughn farm near Rice City, Rhode Island. George A. Dawley is standing in the front yard, his wife; Mercie F. Balley Dawley is looking out the window, and their dog Ben Dawley is on the door step. This house burnt down about 1928."

These two postcards show ice harvesting in the early 1900s. Above, horses wait as a worker loads the wagon with blocks of ice. The worker on the pond has cut the blocks, and the other men bring the blocks to the wagon. On the back of this card below is written, "The location is Fairbanks Corner, at the foot of the hill, in back of Inman's house. Earl Johnson worked there for $2.00 a day cutting ice in 1914." Johnson was a member of the class of 1906 at Rice City School, as seen on page 75.

First Christian Church of Coventry was built in 1846 on Vaughn Hollow Road. When the congregation originally formed in 1813, it was Baptist. In 1881, it changed its affiliation to the United Church of Christ. It gained prominence through the teachings of elder James Burlingame, who presided over the church for more than 50 years. The beautiful interior, seen below in November 2012, still invites the congregation to service each Sunday. The following verse is from "He's Knocking" by Helen O. Larson: "Maybe He is weeping, He's knocked so many times before/ Don't ignore His knocking, For He may not knock no more." (Both, author's collection.)

Elder James Burlingame is seen here in 1850. The leader of the First Christian Church of Coventry, he is the great-great-grandfather of David Underwood. (David Underwood.)

Rev. Fred M. Buker and his family pose for the camera in 1909. Reverend Buker preached at the Rice City Christian Church from 1905 to 1912. In 1929, he was the pastor of the Knotty Oak Baptist Church. In 1938, he was listed as living on the Knotty Oak–to–Hope road.

John Love is seen here in front of the McGregor District School, which was built in 1812 and closed in 1907. Love died in 1918. In 1736, his ancestors Adam and Gabriel Love settled in the area along Great North Road, which was built in 1714. In 1794, it became a toll road and was renamed Plainfield Turnpike.

This 1886 photograph shows the students and teacher at Rice City School. Pictured are, from left to right, (first row) four unidentified students, Annie Spencer, Fannie Barker, and Flora Dawley; (second row) Tom Spencer, Everett Johnson, Virgil Johnson, Will Cahoone, Len Greene, unidentified, James Spencer, Fred Rogers, and Charles Rogers; (third row) Henry Johnson, teacher Hattie Johnson, Ruth Brown, and Nan Taylor. (David Underwood.)

The postcard above shows a class in front of the Rice City School, which was built in 1846 and closed in 1949. It still stands today. A third school, the private Democrat School, was built before 1812 and sold to the public in 1817. The individuals in the postcard below, of a class of Rice City School in 1906, are listed as the Potter family—Ralph, Edward, Perry, E, and Bessie; the Green family—Harold, Henry, Manie, and Mildred; the Kettle family—Alice, M, William, and Thomas; the Scott family—Maude, Cy, and Sam; the Gavitt family—Lottie, Lula, and Mildred; Earl Johnson, and others, with ? Sherry, the teacher.

This postcard view looks west on Plainfield Pike, showing the Rice Tavern on the right. It is said that Samuel Rice christened the tavern on its opening day in 1796. He then declared the area Rice City. In the 1800s, the Danielson stagecoach line maintained an overland route between Providence and Danielson. Rice City was halfway between them, so the stages used the tavern as a stopover to change horses. This also gave passengers a comfortable rest stop. The stage line discontinued service shortly after the trains came to Greene in the 1850s. Later, when automobiles became popular, a gas pump was added in front, at the curb. The following verses are from "The Road of Life" by Helen O. Larson: "The years come and go, as I walk the road of life each day/I will walk this road only once, I'll leave foot prints along the way/And when I reach the end of this road, I will find a peace I never knew/For when I reach the end of this road, my life on Earth will be through."

Isaac Fiske built this one-and-a-half-story house with a side ell (above) in 1890. Included on this Plainfield Pike farm were a blacksmith shop (the small building on the right), a small cottage believed to have been built in 1742, and an outhouse. Fiske was the local blacksmith at this time. Fiske posted this notice (below) after his horse was stolen on July 4, 1907, and offered a reward, giving a Greene address to receive mail. When the railroad bypassed Rice City in 1854 and built its depot in Greene, the post office moved to Greene as well, and Greene took over as the center of local activity.

HORSE STOLEN

On the night of July 4, 1907, red sorrel mare, weight 1,000 lbs., about 15 hands high, black spot on flank big as silver dollar, does not like to put out hind feet, when taken up, cribber, look for scar across tongue.

ISAAC FISKE,

REWARD.   GREENE, R. I.

EZRA D. BATES,

Would respectfully inform his friends and the public generally, that he has now on hand, at his shop, near *Rice City*, a general assortment of

Broadcloths, Cassimeres, Vestings and Trimmings,

of all kinds, which he will sell on the most reasonable terms. A share of public patronage is solicited,

N. B.—Cutting and making Garments executed on the most reasonable terms, and in the most workmanlike manner.

Coventry, April 28, 1841.

Ezra D. Bates published this announcement on April 28, 1841, asking the folks in the area to come to his tailor shop near Rice City. He states that he has a good supply and various assortments of materials and that N.B.—his wife, Nancy Hopkins Bates—makes excellent garments at reasonable rates. They had two children, Lucy and Randall. Nancy passed away in 1873, and Ezra followed her less than a year later, in 1874. The following verse is from "White Satin Gown" by Helen O. Larson: "She put on white satin one day, pink gowns on each bride's maid/She was in Seventh Heaven, All wedding plans had been made/The wedding guests had been invited, the hall was reserved too/Then a few days before the wedding, he told her the wedding was through/He had backed out a few days before, she was left with a broken heart/He said he could never promise, to live till death we do part."

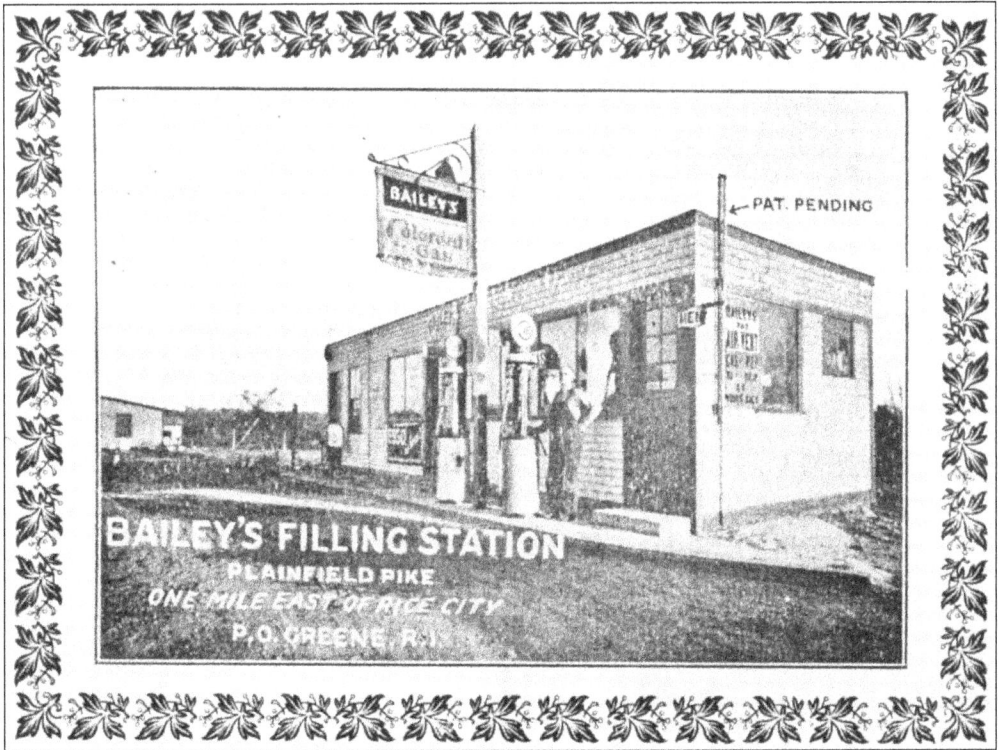

The postcard above shows Bailey's Filling Station on Plainfield Pike. Below, the work crews of Temperance sawmill stop work momentarily to have their photograph taken for this postcard.

A young Abbie M. Fry poses for the camera on Memorial Day in 1910. She went on to graduate from Rhode Island College with a teaching degree. In 1922, she was teaching at Howard Hill School in Foster (see *Foster*, page 103). By 1926, she was teaching in Greene, and she married Lester Underwood that same year. She went on to teach at Western Coventry Grammar School for 30 years before retiring in 1961. After retirement, she maintained the position of school librarian for eight years before becoming the librarian at Greene Public Library. She held that position for the next 15 years before retiring again at age 80. The following verses are from "Lest We Forget" by Helen O. Larson: "When you wave your flag of freedom, let tears fall from your eyes/For the boys who didn't come home, lay in a grave beneath the skies/And as you lay a wreath, on their graves this day/Don't be ashamed to shed some tears, and please take a moment to pray."

This postcard view of the old bridge on Potter Road looks downstream just below the dam seen on the next page. George Vaughn's house was to the right of the span. The bridge washed away in the 1927 flood.

Abbie Fry (later Underwood) poses for the postcard below around 1910. She is standing on the double-span bridge crossing the Moosup River. A tailor shop and a barn are in the left background.

This photograph was taken from the end of the bridge shown on the previous page. The extensions of the bridge railings are seen on both sides of the road leading to George Vaughn's house in 1937. His early-1930s Ford is parked in front.

This 1909 postcard view looks upstream from the bridge towards the Vaughn mill dam and George Vaughn's house and barn. The house was built in the late 1700s, and Vaughn lived there as early as 1851.

Eight

SUMMIT

This postcard shows the railroad coming into Summit from the east. The depot and a boxcar on the siding are seen. In the 1700s, the area was called Perry's Hollow. When the Hartford, Providence & Fishkill Railroad came through, it named its depot Summit because it was built at the highest point on the line. (David Underwood.)

The view of the Summit depot above looks west, with the siding rails on the right. Passengers wait for the train to arrive, and it can be seen approaching from the west. The building on the left had a store and the post office on the first floor. A sign over the door advertises dry goods and groceries, and the sign to the left of the door states there is a Bell telephone inside. The photograph below was taken from almost the same spot, looking in the opposite direction, towards the Coventry Centre depot.

A man sits on the fence beside the Summit depot, patiently awaiting his train. Giles M. Nichols built the general store to the left, seen on the opposite page, in 1856, the same year the depot was constructed.

RAILROAD CROSSING
STOP LOOK AND LISTEN

The view in this postcard, mailed in August 1913, looks north down West Log Bridge Road toward Route 117 and Susan Bowen Road. The building on the right is the current home of Summit General Store (page 96).

This 1911 postcard shows a picnic gathering on the front lawn of Summit Baptist Church. It was built in 1865, and the carriage shed seen in the rear was added at a later date.

This postcard was mailed in August 1913; the view looks west on Main Street in Summit. The building on the far left was constructed by Giles M. Nichols in 1888 and named Nixon's Hall. It later became the Summit Free Library and is now the home of the Coventry Historical Society Museum, which displays documents, photographs, and artifacts from the area. Summit Baptist Church is on the right.

This later photograph shows a number of changes to Summit Baptist Church. A new gable-roofed entryway has been added and an addition has been made to the rear of the church. The carriage shed had to be dismantled. Note the four sets of windows compared to the three sets of window in the photograph on the opposite page. (Henriette Koszela.)

The Summit Sunday school boys' class provided the entertainment for a church program on Friday, August 5, 1898. The boys were James Hopkins, Ernest Green, Charles Tillinghast, Byron Wilcox, Arthur Franklin, and Stephen Capwell. The teacher was Emily Williams. The program was printed in Anthony by Walford B. Read in August 1898.

PROGRAM.

Entertainment

Directed by

The BOYS' CLASS

—— OF THE ——

Summit

Sunday

School.

Friday, August 5, 1898.

This postcard shows William A. Black's general store, on the corner of Main Street and West Log Bridge Road, which was originally built by Giles M. Nichols. Black and his wife, Isabelle, lived on the second floor. The crate on the porch to the left of the left door is from Grocers' Baking Company in Providence.

This early-1900s postcard view looks farther down Main Street as it intersects with West Log Bridge Road. Black's general store is on the left at the corner.

This is a great 1908 view looking east of the railroad. Summit had a blacksmith shop (see below), a sawmill built by James Matteson in 1812, a gristmill, a general store, a train depot, a church, a library, and a few houses. (Donald Carpenter.)

Albert Johnson was the village blacksmith when this early-1900s photograph was taken. At the time, blacksmiths were transitioning from working on horseshoes and carriages to working on automobiles. The vehicle in front has leather seats, fenders, and no top.

Esther (left) and John Koszela Jr. are seen above with Inez Matteson, a family friend, on the Summit rotary in 1937. The view looks west, showing telephone poles along Route 117 in the background. The arrow points north on Route 102. A blinking traffic light can be seen above them. Below, in a view looking east, is the Texaco gas station that Luther Andrews ran in the 1950s, at the intersection of the rotary. The blinking traffic light's shadow is seen on the road in the lower right. (Both, Henriette Koszela.)

The document pictured at right is a 48-page booklet distributed by the Standard Oil Company of New York (Socony) in 1929. It details the history of the company and advertises its products. The back cover text explains how the company is making it easier for pilots to fly. The town or city name was painted in eight-foot white letters on a black background on the roofs of many of the company's buildings in New England and New York. A large white arrow on a black band pointed to the true north position. The markings enabled pilots to ascertain exactly where they were and make corrections and allowances in their navigation as they flew over Soconyland. Pardon Brown passed this booklet out at his Summit Auto Stop station. He is seen below with his team and wagon in front of his station. (Below, Henriette Koszela.)

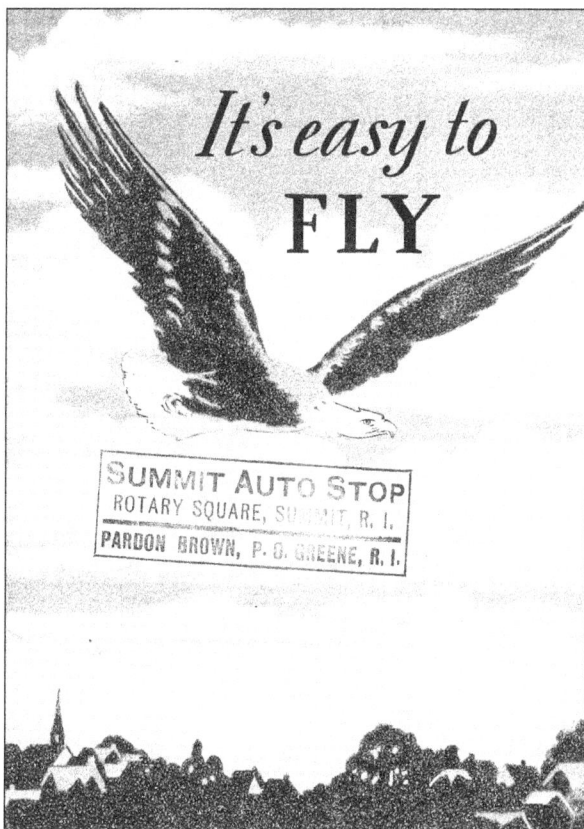

It's easy to FLY

SUMMIT AUTO STOP
ROTARY SQUARE, SUMMIT, R. I.
PARDON BROWN, P. O. GREENE, R. I.

Above, four-year-old John "Sonny" Koszela Jr. proudly displays his tricycle in this 1938 view of the Summit rotary. He is playing in the front yard of the family's lumberyard. Route 102 is headed north behind him, and Route 117 is to the right of the pile of lumber, headed east. Below, his father, John "Jack" Koszela Sr., shows off the 1931 Chevrolet fire engine owned by the Western Coventry Fire District in 1952. The following verse is from "Dedicated to Firemen," written by Helen O. Larson at age 70: "Let's have a large parade, let's tie ribbons on the trees/For what would we ever do, without dedicated men like these." (Both, Henriette Koszela.)

Jack Koszela
1952

Summit School was about a mile east of Summit village on Weeks Hill Road. The rare photograph below shows one of the classes at the school. While the boy in the front center is shoeless, he is at least wearing a sweater. The potbelly stove kept everyone warm in the cold New England winters. Weeks Hill is named for John Wickes Jr., who was the first landowner in the area, in 1728. John Wickes Sr. was one of the 11 men that Samuel Gorton represented when he made the Shawomet Purchase from Miantonomi, the chief sachem of the Narragansett Indians, in January 1643. (Both, Henriette Koszela.)

Maxwell Mays was born in Providence on August 13, 1918. In 1941, he graduated from the Rhode Island School of Design and bought 295 acres of woods in Coventry. He joined the Air Force in 1942 and was stationed in Brazil, where he began his painting career. After the war, he returned to his secluded 1737 farmhouse to continue his painting. (Western Rhode Island Civic and Historical Society.)

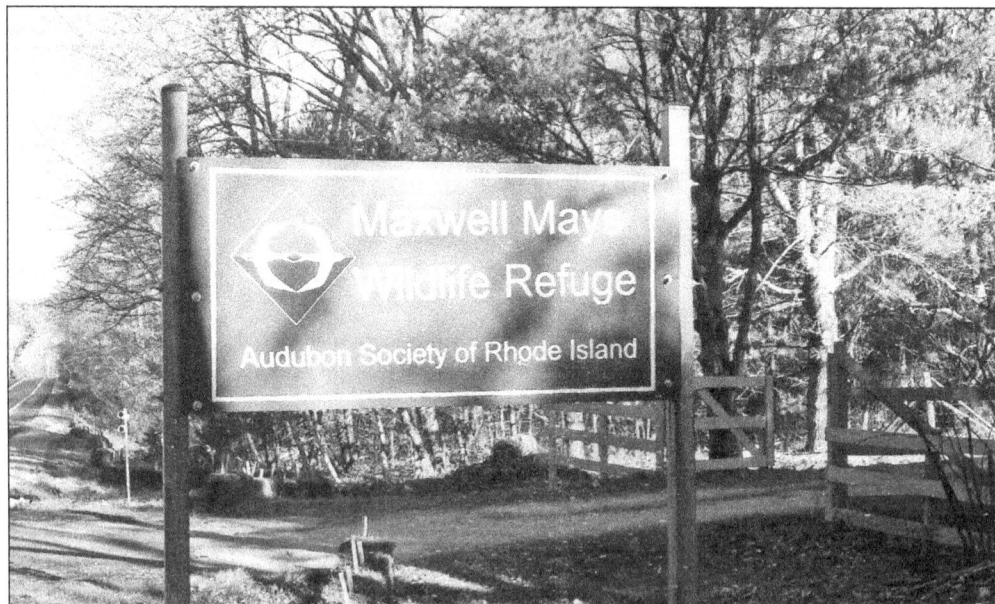

In 2001, Maxwell Mays donated his 295-acre refuge to the Audubon Society of Rhode Island. It is now the Maxwell Mays Wildlife Refuge, on Route 102. He was quoted as saying, "I would like this land to stay open; I would like this land to breathe." He passed away on November 16, 2009, at the age of 91. He will always be remembered as a renowned painter of the villages of Coventry. (Author's collection.)

In 1990, the Coventry Historical Society wanted to publish a book celebrating the 250th anniversary of Coventry, the following year. The Hoechst Celanese Corporation of Coventry agreed to sponsor the project and commissioned Maxwell Mays to create the cover image. Mays said, "I chose the Anthony Mill scene because you have the train, the mill, and the river. These were the three most important things in Coventry." (Coventry Historical Society.)

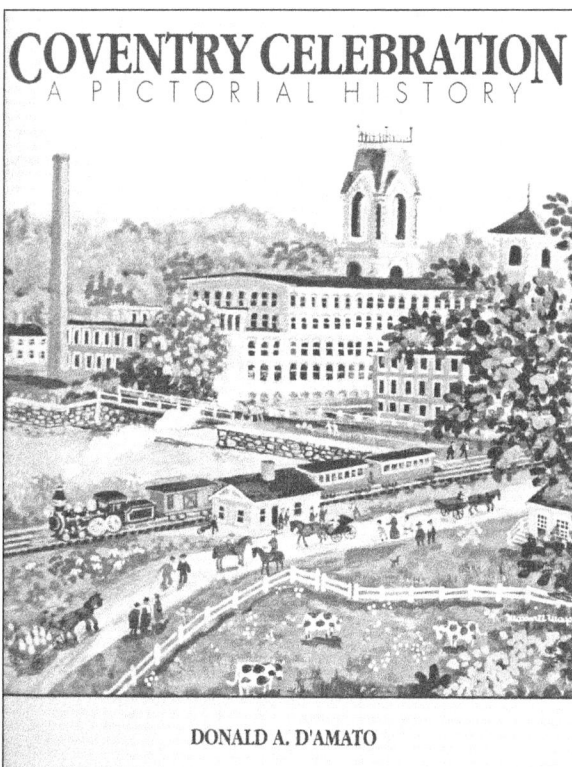

COVENTRY CELEBRATION
A PICTORIAL HISTORY

DONALD A. D'AMATO

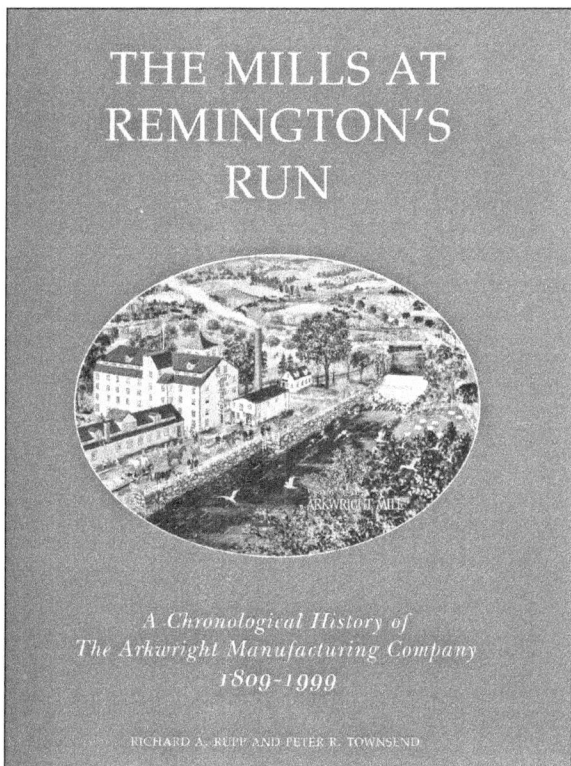

THE MILLS AT REMINGTON'S RUN

A Chronological History of
The Arkwright Manufacturing Company
1809-1999

RICHARD A. RUPP AND PETER R. TOWNSEND

In 1990, Arkwright Manufacturing Company celebrated 180 years of continuous manufacturing. Maxwell Mays unveiled a painting of what the mill looked like in 1885, which inspired this book, *The Mills At Remington's Run*. In 1999, after a lot of research, the history of the Arkwright Manufacturing Company was published by two 20-year employees, Richard P. Rupp and Peter R. Townsend. (Author's collection.)

This aerial view looks south on Route 102, where the Summit rotary used to be. It was taken in the mid-1970s when the intersection of Routes 117 and 102 was reconstructed. The State of Rhode Island built the sand dome on the right in 1988. It is on the lot where Pardon Brown operated Summit Auto Stop. Koszela's Lumber is on the left. (Henriette Koszela.)

The sign for Olde Summit Village welcomes visitors to the community. It proudly advertises Summit General Store, "Rhode Island's Only Real General Store." (Author's collection.)

Nine

TIOGUE, SPRING LAKE, AND MAPLE ROOT

Christopher Varrica is seen here fishing on Lake Tiogue on the morning of June 20, 2012. An inscription on the 1976 memorial reads, "Korea-Vietnam Veterans Memorial Park, To honor all who died, are missing in action, or were wounded and those who served their country to keep America free so that we might enjoy peace through their heroism." (Author's collection.)

This group of boys poses for a photograph while playing hockey on a sunny but cold winter day on Lake Tiogue.

Margarite Rinfret (left) and Rita Blair (later Kenyon), the daughter of Alphee Blair, stand on frozen Lake Tiogue behind "Kid" Blair's Showboat Restaurant in the early 1940s. (Gail Mitchell Slezak.)

This postcard shows "Kid" Blair's Showboat Restaurant as seen from Tiogue Avenue (Route 3), which was the main route from Boston to New York at the time. Blair advertised a $2.25 smorgasbord on Sundays from 12:00 p.m. to 9:00 p.m. The Showboat also had air-conditioned party and banquet facilities for 200. (Coventry Historical Society.)

This photograph, taken on February 21, 1943, shows a smiling Helen Rekas on the rear steps of the Showboat, which lead down to the lake. The Showboat burned down on January 16, 1976, and was never rebuilt. (Gail Mitchell Slezak.)

Rinfret's Cabins

Screened Porches - Showers - Radio

ACROSS FROM KID BLAIR'S SHOWBOAT
ON THE LAKE

Swimming - Dining - Dancing

ROUTE 3   TIOGUE LAKE   WASHINGTON, R. I.

This postcard advertises the Rinfret family cabins, on Route 3 across from "Kid" Blair's Showboat Restaurant, where people went for swimming, dining, and dancing. Arthur and Bernadette Rinfret bought seven lots for $1,000 and built the cabins, a house, and a diner next door. Bernadette was expecting her fifth child, Claudette, when her husband passed away at age 41. (Gail Mitchell Slezak.)

The cabins, which were located behind Rinfret's home and office and Bernie's Diner, have all been converted to permanent housing and are seen here in July 2012. (Author's collection.)

Rinfret's Cabins and Bernie's Diner were family businesses where everyone chipped in and did his or her share. Here, in the early 1940s, after Arthur Rinfret passed away, 13-year-old Jean Rinfret stands on a ladder to paint a window on one of the cabins. The following verses are from "A Place Called Home" by Helen O. Larson: "Though it's only a shack, weather beaten and worn/ It's a place that she calls home, it's a shelter when in a storm/Maybe it needs painting, and a new roof too/But it is a place so restful, when the day is through/Just to sit by the old wood stove, and see the flames rise high/It's the most restful place, beneath the blue and white sky/Just to rest in bed at night, with a homemade quilt on the bed/It's so peaceful and homey, she wouldn't trade for a mansion instead." (Gail Mitchell Slezak.)

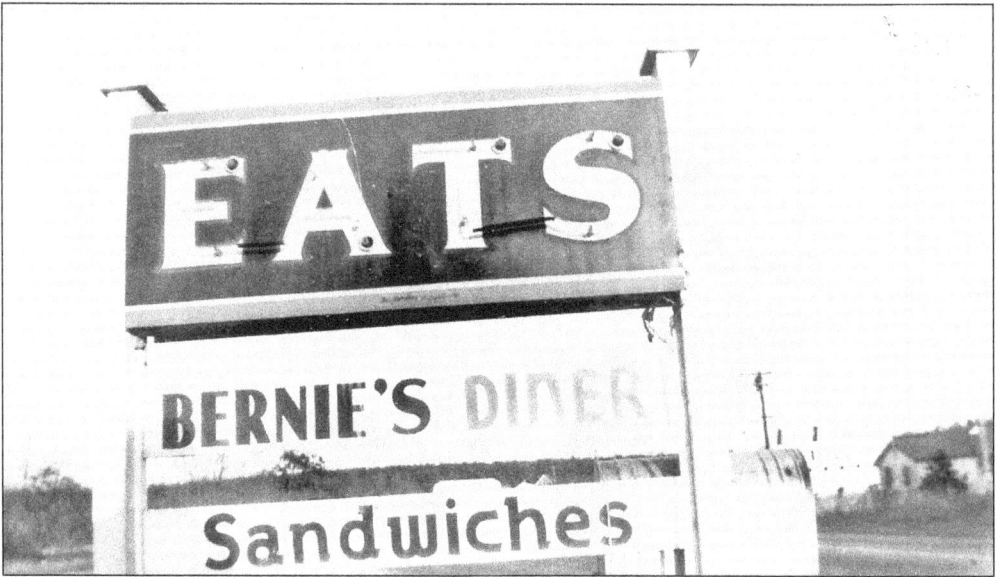

Arthur Rinfret named Bernie's Diner for his wife, Bernadette. It later became Joe's Diner. All of the Rinfret children, Pauline, Margarite, Jean, Richard, and Claudette, worked in the diner. This sign stood above their mailbox. (Gail Mitchell Slezak.)

The reverse of this 1950s postcard indicates it is Joe's Diner on Route 3 across from Tiogue Lake. The text proudly claims, "We serve real home cooking, top quality, top quantity at reasonable prices." The place mat shows that it is only a short drive from Providence.

Joe's Diner later became Joe's Family Restaurant, as this postcard from the 1960s shows. The back of this postcard indicates that it is "located in the Lace Center of America" and advertises superb cocktails in the "Towne Room Lounge."

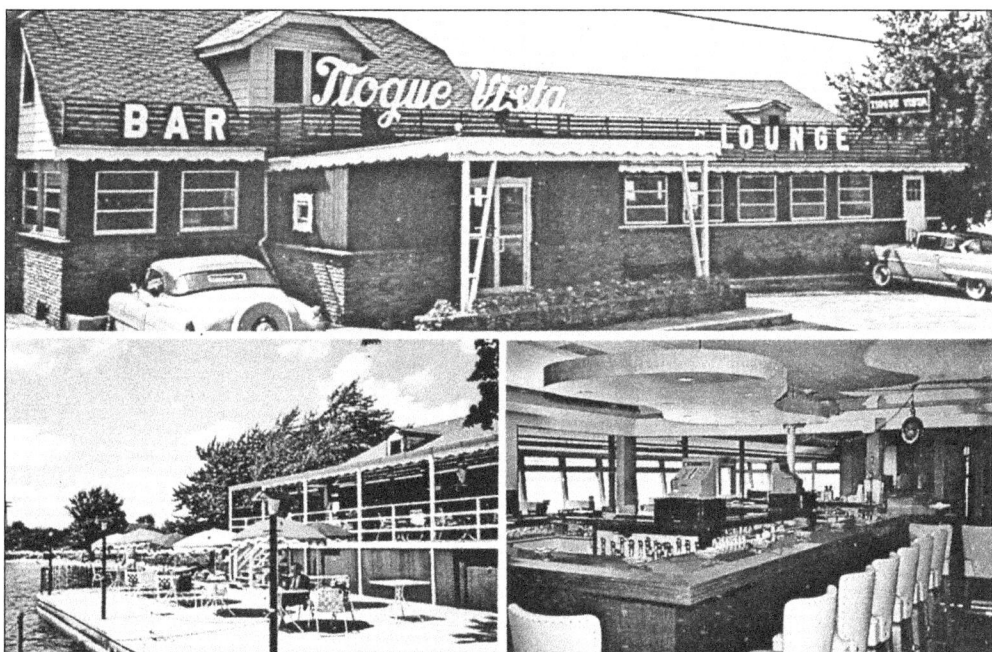

The Tiogue Vista was just down the street from Joe's, right on Lake Tiogue. This postcard shows the front, the lakefront patio behind the lounge, and the bar. The back reads, "Ample facilities for banquets, weddings, parties, and special groups up to 400. Open year round, your host, Reggie LaFleur." (Dean Bentley.)

Peter Stevens was five years old when his parents, Howard and Luella, started the *Coventry Reminder* at the kitchen table in 1953. It was initially four pages. For many years, Peter and his siblings Amey and Mark stapled and placed stamps on the issues for mailing. By the time of this issue, in 1956, it had grown to six pages. It became a tabloid in the 1970s and, today, 60 years after it was founded, it has been divided into two sections. This issue's cover features Webber Motor Sales, before it became Webber Chevrolet, which was owned and operated by Marvin Webber on Tiogue Avenue. Before the dealership sold Chevrolets, it sold Studebakers and Packards. The $595 weekly special was a 1953 Willys that had two doors and "R-H"—a radio and a heater, which were options at the time.

The postcard above shows the one-room Spring Lake School around 1905. The back of the card indicates that it was located "on the corner of Reservoir Road." The photograph below was taken by Fred Anthony. The mill was in the vicinity of the present McDonald's. Ezra Ramsdell built the first mill there in 1818, which burned in 1830. It was replaced by a second mill, which also burned, in 1906.

Seen here in 2012, this house is known as the George Taylor house. It has had a number of additions through the years and is the last standing house of Spring Lake. (Author's collection.)

Walter and Letha Sodergren purchased this building in 1952 and opened the Maple Root Exchange. He bought and sold antiques and furniture, and she started collecting and selling lamps. When Walter passed away in 1964, Letha continued running the store. This 1959 photograph shows a woman about to enter a 1951 Buick Roadmaster with her newfound treasure. (Courtesy of Phyllis Sodergren-Houston.)

Letha M. Sodergren opened her own shop on November 8, 1968. She ran it with daughter Phyllis until she retired 26 years later, on October 29, 1994. At right, the Candle Snuffer sign proudly hangs from a lamppost. The open gate welcomed friends and strangers to the Sodergrens' lamp shop. Below, Letha Sodergren holds a painting of her shop as she sits surrounded by her beloved lamps. The poem on page 8 celebrates the shop. (Both, Phyllis Sodergren-Houston.)

This 1908 postcard shows the Maple Root Baptist Church and its carriage house. It was built in 1797, but the society was first organized in 1762, with 26 members. By 1782, they had increased to 75. Pardon Tillinghast assumed charge of the society in 1811 and built the membership to 180. By 1815, it had reached 300; in 1821, it was 400; and it topped out around 600 before groups began to break away. One group of 47 members started the Coventry Central Six Principles Baptist Meeting House (Knotty Oak Church). Below, the members attend a church picnic in 1911.

Aug. 12, 1911

Ten

WASHINGTON
AND COLVINTOWN

This photograph of the Paine House was taken in 2012. Some believe the original section was built in 1668, and deeds have been traced back to 1691. Francis Brayton either built it or put an addition on it in 1748. In 1785, it was home to the Brayton Tavern. Later, it became the Holden Tavern. The house is named for Herbert Paine. In 1953, Zilpha W. Foster bequeathed it to the Western Rhode Island Civic Historical Society, which now maintains it as a museum that is open to the public. (Author's collection.)

The Paine House has many rooms, including the parlor (above), where visitors could relax and socialize with other guests. The following verses are from "Gingerbread Clock" by Helen O. Larson: "I have an old gingerbread clock, it sits on a shelf in my den/It belonged to a dear old couple long ago, I wish I could of known them then/As I wind the clock each day, to picture these people I try/These dear old folks, that lived in days gone by." The keeping room (below) is where guests were served their meals. (Both, author's collection.)

This room is called the wedding room. The cape hanging on the pole was made for Eunice Birther Clarke. "Gingerbread Clock" continues: "I wonder if the husband, would wind the clock each night/I wonder if his wife would say, Pa, don't wind the clock to tight/I wonder if they would sit, in their old rocking chairs/And when the clock struck ten, they would slowly climb the stairs." The room below is called the travelers' room. Each room is complete with period furnishings. (Both, author's collection.)

These 10 beautiful ladies, dressed in period fashion, pose during an event at the Paine House, at 7 Station Street. This verse is the conclusion of "Gingerbread Clock": "As I glance at the clock again, memories of these folks it does bring/Their beautiful gingerbread clock, could grace the home of a king." (Coventry Historical Society.)

Charles A. Foster's business sign hangs in the barn behind Paine House. He resided in the house until 1875, at which time his parents, John and Harriet Foster, built a home next door. In 1958, at the age of 95, Charles was the recipient of the Boston Post Cane (see *Pawtuxet Valley Villages*, page 120). He passed away on April 21, 1961, at the age of 99. (Author's collection.)

This is an 1892 portrait of Charles A. Foster's wife, Zilpha W. Johnson Foster. She not only bequeathed the Paine House to the local historical society, but she also left land on Knotty Oak Road for a bird sanctuary. In 1957, the town constructed the new Coventry High School on the property. Today, it is Alan Shawn Feinstein Middle School. (Western Rhode Island Civic and Historical Society.)

Zilpha W. Foster (far left) and her husband, Charles A. Foster (third from left), enjoy a bicycle ride with some friends, perhaps on a Sunday. This was a time when most people wore their Sunday best for every activity. This image is also on the cover. (Coventry Historical Society.)

This beautiful hand-wound clock is displayed in the Paine House. It is the original clock used by stationmaster John Manchester at the Washington railroad station. When passenger service to Washington was suspended, Manchester rescued the clock and gave it to the Paine House. (Western Rhode Island Civic and Historical Society.)

This is an original ticket for the New York, New Haven & Hartford Railroad, dated 1912 on the back. It was good for one fare between Centreville and Washington at half price. It indicates that the railroad's liability limit for lost luggage is $50. (Henriette Koszela.)

These two documents are from the Read schoolhouse, built in 1831. The image at right shows a textbook, S.S. Cornell's revised edition of his second part of a systematic series of school geographies. It was published in 1872 and used at the Read school. The image below is of the diploma of Harold Lester Warner, which was awarded to him on June 24, 1926, for completing the course of study presented by the grammar school department. There is a plaque hanging on the wall under Warner's framed diploma in the Read schoolhouse. It states, "Harold Lester Warner was the only graduate from Read School in 1926." (Both, Coventry Historical Society.)

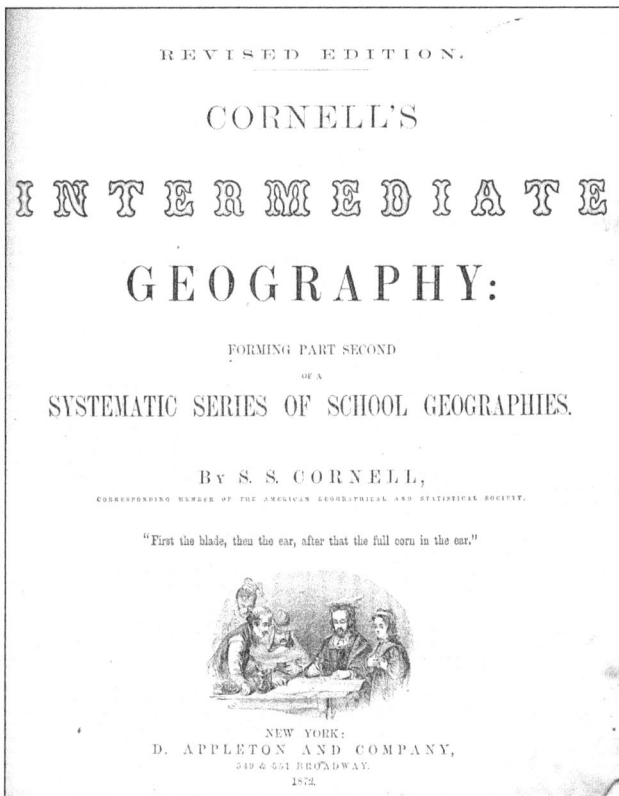

REVISED EDITION.

CORNELL'S

INTERMEDIATE

GEOGRAPHY:

FORMING PART SECOND
OF A
SYSTEMATIC SERIES OF SCHOOL GEOGRAPHIES.

By S. S. CORNELL,
CORRESPONDING MEMBER OF THE AMERICAN GEOGRAPHICAL AND STATISTICAL SOCIETY.

"First the blade, then the ear, after that the full corn in the ear."

NEW YORK:
D. APPLETON AND COMPANY,
549 & 551 BROADWAY.
1872.

This photograph was discovered in a drawer of a cabinet at the Paine House. The caption on the back reads, "This is Mrs. John Randall [Eva M.] with her three older children. They are left to right, Lester, Hazel, and Flora." (Western Rhode Island Civic and Historical Society.)

The postcard below shows the Smith House, on the corner of Station and Park Streets. The residence was originally built for Dr. Allen Tillinghast, whose daughter Evangeline married Dr. Frank Bailey Smith and lived in the home with him. The house has since been converted to apartments.

Dr. Frank Bailey Smith was born in Columbus, Georgia, on January 3, 1853. After completing public school and college preparation, he studied with Dr. William Lewis of Moosup, Connecticut, for three years. He graduated from the University of New York's medical department in 1873. He began his practice in Coventry that same year. In 1879, he married Evangeline H. Tillinghast, the daughter of Dr. Allen Tillinghast.

Dr. Allen Tillinghast was born on May 20, 1798, in West Greenwich, Rhode Island. On August 28, 1817, he married Mercy Lillibridge. After acquiring his degree in medicine, he settled in Coventry. The card below is a pass to admit him to the lectures at the Berkshire Medical Institution on August 4, 1842. He died at the age of 81 on December 30, 1879.

BERKSHIRE MEDICAL INSTITUTION.

Admit Mr. *Allen Tillinghast,*

TO THE LECTURES ON

THEORY AND PRACTICE OF MEDICINE AND OBSTETRICS.

H. H. Childs,

Pittsfield, August 4th, 1842.

This train has just left the Washington station and is on the way to the next stop, Anthony, and points east. The Knotty Oak Cemetery, on the corner of Routes 116 and 117 is in the distance under the railroad bridge. (Henriette Koszela.)

Rev. Benjamin Moone's mill was built in 1859. In 1874, he paid $37.50 in taxes on the mill, which was valued at $7,500. It was on Washington Street opposite Station Street. The mill burned down on February 12, 1907. This photograph was taken in 1891. (Western Rhode Island Civic and Historical Society.)

The postcard above was mailed in 1929. It shows the Livingston Woolen Mill in Washington. The road in front is now Route 117. South Main Street is on the left, between the tree and the mill. The image was taken before the trolley tracks were removed and a traffic light was installed. The interior of the mill is seen below in the 1920s. A few workers, along with supervisor Ralph Emerson Chase (far right, wearing a vest), have stopped to pose for the camera. (Both, Coventry Historical Society.)

The Coventry Sea Scouts are seen above in 1941. They are lined up in front of a restaurant on Main Street, where Coventry Shopper's Park is today. The building to the left housed Shippee's Variety Store, which advertised Warwick Club Beverages. Everett Hudson Sr. bought Shippee's Variety Store from Ed Shippee in 1942 and renamed it Hudson Variety. On April 26, 1947, he bought the building next door, seen below, and moved his business there. (Above, Coventry Historical Society; below, Everett Hudson Jr.)

The photograph above was taken in January 1950 after Everett Hudson Sr. had remodeled his store. He decided to rename it Hudson's because that was already what everyone called it. Below, Charles Watson used to open the store for the Hudsons at 6:00 a.m. and stay until 10:00 a.m., when Hudson would take over. Hudson would stay until 2:00 p.m., when his wife, Mae, took over until closing at 6:00 p.m. The Hudsons ran the store until 1966, when they retired. On the counter to the right of Watson is a box of Dorsey Cigars for 10¢ each. (Both, Everett Hudson Jr.)

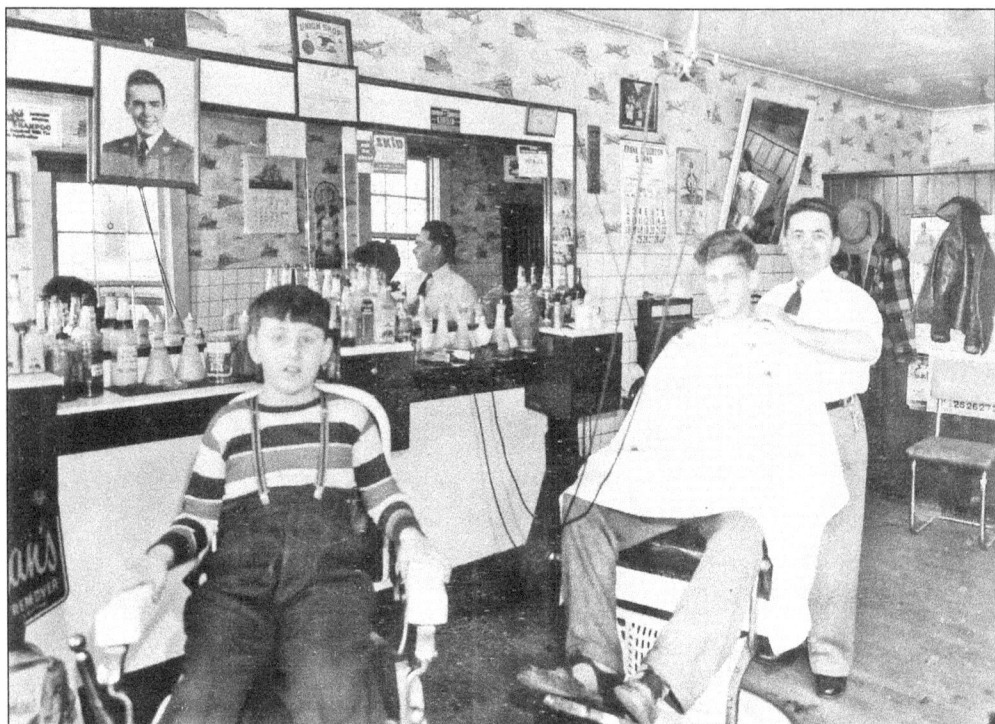

Arthur "Shorty" Labrie is seen above in his place of business, Shorty's Barber Shop, in 1951. As a young boy, the author had his hair cut at Shorty's. The building, on Main Street, is only 11 feet wide and 20 feet long and was built around 1780. At one time, it was the office for the stables next door. Labrie's son Richard was in the Air Force in the 1950s, and Shorty proudly displayed his picture. Richard began cutting hair when he was 15 and continued working with his father after returning from the Korean War. He maintained the business after Shorty's retirement in 1968. At left, Arthur Olney (left) and Shorty take a break at a business across the street. A poster advertises that the Royal International Circus is coming to Coventry on Friday, July 20, 1956. (Left, Ricky Labrie.)

1776 INDEPENDENCE DAY. 1882

GRAND CELEBRATION

— AT —

WASHINGTON VILLAGE !

Oration, Music, Clambake,

BASE BALL,

Tight Rope Walking,
Clay Pigeon Shooting,
Grand Swimming Match,
Tub Race, Sack Race,
Running Race, Three Legged Race,

Balloon Ascension, Illuminations, Fire Works,

&c., &c., &c.

PROGRAMME.

Ringing of Bells and National Salute at sunrise, noon and sunset.

8 o'clock—Grand Parade of Antiques, Horribles, Lunatics, Sorrowfuls, and Block Island Guards. Four Bands of Music in the line. Route of march: Washington to Quidnick, Quidnick to Crompton, Crompton to Centreville, Centreville to Arctic Centre, Arctic Centre to Quidnick, Quidnick to Washington. Every one intending to parade with these organizations are requested to report at head-quarters at 7 1-2 o'clock, sharp.

11 o'clock—An Oration will be delivered, and Speaking by several prominent citizens of Coventry.

1 o'clock—The Clambake will be opened, and the Chowder served with Cake, Coffee, &c.

2 o'clock—Sack Race, Running Race, and the celebrated Three-Legged Race. These races are open to all.

2½ o'clock—Base Ball Game by two celebrated nines.

3 o'clock—Clay Pigeon Shooting by the Coventry Gun Club. Open to all shooters.

4 o'clock—Tub Race and Swimming Match. These races are open to all.

5 o'clock—Walking the Tight Rope across the Pawtuxet river, by Prof. J. E. Holmes.

The Steamer Ideal, the smallest steamer in the world has been refitted and will make excursions from the wharf west of Washington Mill to the Picnic Grounds.

Dancing after 3 o'clock P. M. in a large tent erected for the purpose.

In the evening a grand Illumination of the Pawtuxet River and a Balloon Ascension; Mighty Volcanic Eruption and Burning of the Gaspee.

Ice Cream and other Refreshments will sold on the grounds.

Come one, Come all and hear the Cannon Roar, the Eagle Scream and participate in the Grandest Celebration ever witnessed on the Globe.

PER ORDER COMMITTEE OF ARRANGEMENTS.

Rhode Island Democrat Print, Providence.

This 1882 Washington village document is quite fragile. It announces the "Grand Celebration" of Independence Day on July 4, 1882. The program states that the day will include the "Ringing of Bells and National Salute at sunrise, noon, and sunset." Four bands led a grand parade at 8:00 a.m., which began in Washington and proceeded to Quidnick, Crompton, Centreville, Arctic Centre, Quidnick, and then end back in Washington. Several prominent citizens of Coventry spoke at 11:00 a.m. Chowder and clam cakes were served at 1:00 p.m. From 1:00 p.m. to 5:00 p.m. there were all kinds of activities, including sack races, a baseball game, a clay pigeon shoot, and tub races. At 5:00 p.m., professor J.E. Holmes walked a tightrope across the Pawtuxet River. The evening ended with a "Grand Illumination of the Pawtuxet River and a Balloon Ascension, Mighty Volcano Eruption, and Burning of the Gaspee." The program ends with: "Come one, Come all and hear the Cannon Roar, the Eagle Scream, and participate in the Grandest Celebration ever witnessed on the Globe."

Annie Nestel was born in 1880 in New Bedford, Massachusetts. Michael Wolf was born in 1867 in the city of Ulm on the banks of the Danube River in Germany. In 1887, at the age of 20, Wolf came to America and settled in New Bedford. He married Nestel in 1899. In 1921, he bought a 22-acre farm in Colvintown. This is their wedding portrait. (Courtesy of Leisa Jorgensen.)

Michael and Annie Wolf, the author's grandparents, raised six children on the farm. The postcard below shows their son Louis in his store, Wolf's Hall of Taxidermy, in 1949. He started taxidermy as a hobby, but ended up making a living from it for more than 60 years. He mounted everything, from a small boy's trout to Admiral Byrd's lead sled dog to the turtle on the opposite page.

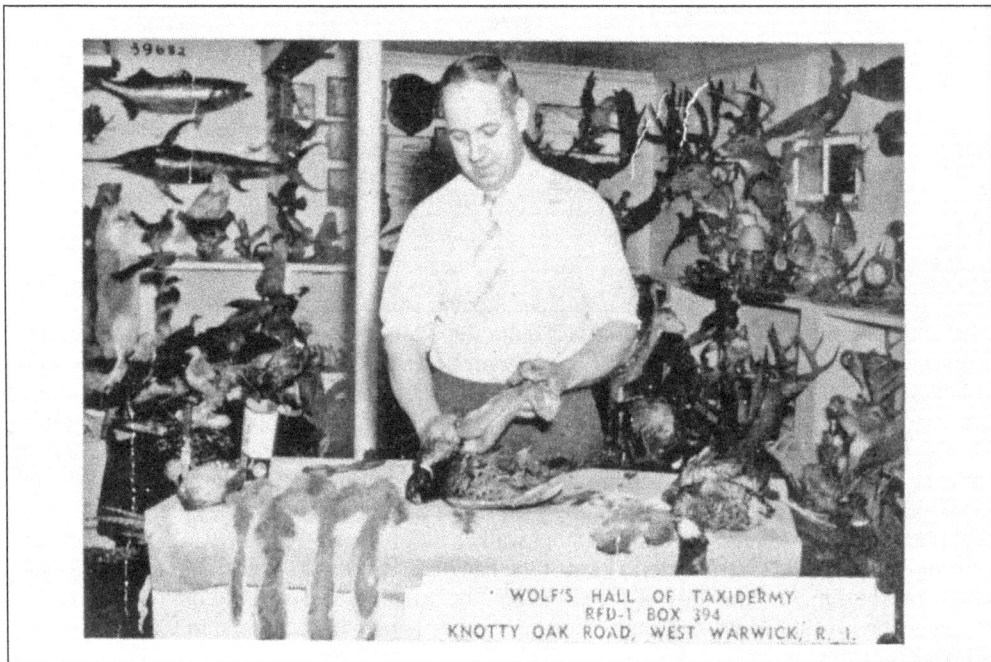

WOLF'S HALL OF TAXIDERMY
RFD-1 BOX 394
KNOTTY OAK ROAD, WEST WARWICK, R. I.

On July 2, 1952, Everett Webster and Bill Tucker, both of Peacedale, fished for blues 18 miles off the coast of Newport. What they caught instead was this 1,750-pound leatherback turtle. They then bought the hearse below and toured the country with the turtle. For 50¢, people could view the "World's Largest Leather Back Turtle." Louis Wolf spent 48 hours mounting the turtle and also painted the scene of the ocean seen behind it above. This was a skill he learned at the Swain School of Design in New Bedford, Massachusetts. Wolf's son Normand started working with him when he was nine and has carried on the business to this day. (Both, Normand D. Wolf.)

The American Legion locomotive above is also seen on page 26 in *Pawtuxet Valley Villages*. It was built to symbolize the train that pulled boxcars in France during World Wars I and II. The boxcars were originally built between 1865 and 1885 to haul freight. During the wars, they were converted to carry either 40 men or 8 horses to the front lines. The author discovered the engine resting in Coventry in December 2012. It is patiently waiting to have work done to its engine. The outfit at left was worn by an American Legion member during parades, when Legionnaires stood on the platform in the rear and tossed candy to the children lining the streets. (Both, author's collection.)

This restored Rhode Island boxcar from the Merci Train is displayed at the Museum of Work and Culture in Woonsocket. In 1948, France wanted to thank America for its assistance during World Wars I and II, so the French sent a gesture of gratitude to the United States. The response from the people of war-ravaged France was so enthusiastic that 49 boxcars were filled with an overflow of gifts. On February 3, 1949, the restored boxcars—one for each state and one to be shared between the territory of Hawaii and the District of Columbia—arrived in New York Harbor aboard the French freighter *Magellan*. It was called the Merci Train. The bronze plaque on the lower left front of the boxcar reads, "Boxcar used in the 1st World War, presented by the French National Railroads to the State of Rhode Island in gratitude for the help given to France by the American people." (Author's collection.)

Visit us at
arcadiapublishing.com

www.ingramcontent.com/pod-product-compliance
Lightning Source LLC
Chambersburg PA
CBHW080616110426
42813CB00006B/1524